DEEP DOWN

Colin King

A Grampians Murder Mystery

Deep Down is the third of four regional murder mystery novels written by Colin King. Colin lives in Bendigo as well as spending time at the writing bolt hole he built in Grampians bushland. In pre-author life, he directed major government projects.

Other novels and praise

A VINTAGE DEATH
WETLAND
WIRE AND BONE

'It's extraordinary.'
'An amazing book based around the Grampians.'
The ABC

'It's a ripping yarn, full of greed, violent death, jealousy, and a smattering of sex. Oh, and lots of wine, of course.'
Max Allen, The Australian

'Here is an author who knows and loves his Australia … with an excursion through painful family secrets on the way to solving a baffling crime.'
Tony Wright, from The Age

'King understands perfectly Central Victoria's potential for a ripper read.'
'A suspenseful novel which is both surprising and satisfying.'
Dianne Dempsey, author, reviewer for The Age

'A great read set in a captivating corner of Australia.'
Adam McNicol, author, The Mallee: A journey through North-west Victoria.

CONTENTS

Deep Down first published by Shawline Publishing Group 2022
Dying for a Coffee,first published by Accidental Publishing 2019
This edition published by Glovebox Publishing 2025

 ColinKingAuthor/

ISBN 978-1-7642005-0-9

Cover design by Jaqui Lynch, Preloaded Design
Cover photo of Mount Abrupt by Matt Tiffen

The author and the publisher have made every effort to contact copyright holders for material used in this book. Any person or organisation that may have been overlooked should contact the publisher.

Glove Box Publishing
PO Box 285 Strathdale Vic 3550 Australia
vintagestaff@hotmail.com

DEEP DOWN

For Caiden, Logan, Nahlo, Bailey and Harry

Chapter 1

Tahlia Lock watched Terry raise the lid on a jewellery box, millions of years in the making. Its outer form of freshly excavated stone resembled a misshapen cricket ball sitting weightily in his palm. A jagged circumference crack allowed the stone's two halves to be parted and re-aligned with jigsaw puzzle perfection. Such a conducive split stemmed from a single masterful blow. The trick was to land the hammer without shattering the shell of ancient cooled lava in the process. The prize for keeping both hemispheres intact was two quartz-encrusted hollows of a thunderegg. For the lucky, the glistening void also housed long-incubated bounty. Terry's egg was thus fertile. The prehistoric womb had utilised every intervening eon to cultivate a flawless black crystal.

Terry shifted his grip to part the pale stone's halves like a ring-box being opened at a marriage proposal — on this occasion, with un-bended knee. He had unearthed and cracked the egg that morning to divulge, extricate and ponder its lustrous treasure. Then, as was his usual practice at the diggings, he returned the pearl to its shell — so to speak — for safekeeping. A layer of pliant mud added to the egg's inner void served as bush cotton wool.

Tahlia leaned forward and strained her gaze at a large quartz gemstone resting in the snug bed of its creation. Half mud-encrusted, yet undeniably beautiful.

'Wow … I mean WOW. It's brill. I love the colour.'

''course you do,' Terry said.

Tahlia instinctively diverted a wary eye in Terry's direction. On this occasion, her radar was indifferent, letting doubt override being affronted by ostensible inference about her Aboriginality.

'Yeah', Terry continued, un-affronted by her glower. 'They call it smoky quartz, but this one's dead-set black. Should be worth a bit more, I reckon.'

Her gaze locked back on the gemstone.

'And it's so perfect.'

'Pretty much. Mother nature doesn't usually do as good a job as a Belgian gem cutter. But this one's as precise as you get off the bat.'

'Can I take it out?'

'Sure. I just store them like that 'til I get home, so they don't get knocked around in the ute. Most people don't bother.'

Tahlia picked it up as carefully as she might handle an injured butterfly and placed it gently onto her palm.

'Here, let me get some of that mud off for you.'

Terry grabbed the stone without ceremony and began rubbing it firmly on his crumpled, dry-mud encrusted shorts. It was the only garment he wore, along with boots and whatever underpants he may or may not have on. His meagre wardrobe and the rest of his being, including his feral hair and beard, bore an orange-ish patina that matched the mounds of extracted soil they stood amongst. The shorts nevertheless had the capacity to absorb an additional skerrick of mud, allowing Terry to present the gem anew in untarnished glory. To demonstrate a point, he held it at head height between the tips of his forefinger and thumb. The hexagonal prism was about four centimetres long and pared to a pencillike point at both ends. An array of glossy facets offered tiny windows into an underlying blackness.

'That's what they call a Herkimer diamond. See, it's formed with a diamond-shaped tip at both ends.'

He cocked his head to examine his own claim, then moved it close to Tahlia's face for her appreciation.

As Tahlia focussed, Terry noticed her eyes matched the gem's dark translucence.

'Matches your eyes,' he uttered as a revelation to himself.

'Yeah? Thanks.'

Detective Sergeant Rory James — the other in the gathering of three — was drawn closer to see for himself.

'What's it worth?' he asked.

'Ahh … there it is,' Terry said, raising both hands and bowing his head in the manner of feigning modesty. 'Always the first question. Never fails.'

5

The intimation of dollars outweighing his appreciation of its splendour stung enough for Rory to dig in. He locked his best stare on Terry before delivering a comeback.

'So, you just go to all this trouble …' he nodded towards the mineshaft and the immense piles of clay that had been painstakingly removed by hand, '… to put them on your mantlepiece for show. Or do you chuck them back in the hole like undersized fish?'

Terry was proving impervious to reproach. He took it as a genuine question and laughed.

'Yeah, nah. I know this looks like a crazy way to spend your day … on purpose,' he added and laughed again at his own joke. 'But it's a collector thing. A bug. The thrill of the hunt. You find a rich gemstone fossicker, and I guarantee he never found his fortune at the bottom of a hole in the ground. He only made his money so he could afford to spend time digging one of these holes. Alright, it is an actual hunt for treasure, I'll give you that …' he responded to an imagined argument, '… but the carrot isn't money.

'Having said all that, you can get a quid or two for them. Something like this beauty, I reckon I could get anything from twenty bucks to five hundred if I play it right.'

'Are you serious? How can it vary that much?'

'I blame the internet … and marketing. I mean, smoky quartz was always pretty passé at lapidary club meets. Still is, pretty much. But nowadays, on the world-wide-web, these things have become all-conquering crystals with powers. You're talking hundreds of dollars. If you believe people on Instagram, one of these little beauties can dissolve energy fields and fix just about everything. Depression, infertility, moodiness, anger … resentment …' He started to slow down, but not for long. '… emotional balance, nerves, headaches, cramps. You can even enhance your clairvoyant ability, presuming you have some. No shit. This is the crap you have to wade through if you search online about the stuff.'

Rory gave an acknowledging nod of having been enlightened.

'What about using it for jewellery?' Tahlia asked.

'Yeah. I've seen them used as pendants and stuff. Just find yourself a jeweller who knows how to fasten and mount something out of the ordinary like this, and Bob's your uncle.'

'No need. I'd glue it with resin from a grass tree like that,' she pointed to one of the kangaroo tail xanthorrhoea plants on the edge of the surrounding scrub.

'Mix that resin with charcoal or native bee wax. Worked alright for the last forty thousand years.'

Rory had picked up a fair bit about Tahlia on their drive to the gemstone site and was still not failing to be impressed when she espoused her Indigenous knowledge. Terry looked to Rory for a lead. It was dawning on him that undersized Tahlia, who was dressed in an oversized Parks Victoria uniform, was here for a purpose. His mind raced.

They can't be thinking there's an Aboriginal connection to what I've stumbled across, can they? Even if they're wrong, which they fucking well are, something like that could put the kybosh on my dig for fuck knows how long.

Tahlia filled the pause. She pulled a thin leather neck band from beneath her shirt. It held a shaped-shell pendant mounted imperceptibly onto an elegant matt black square of hitherto undeterminable material.

'See. Only two years old but still going strong.'

She beamed a wide smile.

'That kangaroo leather too?' Terry said, hazarding a calculated it-might-be-best-to-keep-on-side kind of guess.

'Emu.'

'Ah.'

Not knowing where else to tread on the subject, Terry turned to Rory. There was no lifeline on offer.

'Okay. Show me the body,' Rory said.

Chapter 2

YESTERDAY

'I've got Damon Rich on the line. Wants a chat. Are you in?'

Fran, PA for Homicide's Inspector Richard Bourke, was leaning into his office doorway. Bourke leant back from his computer keyboard, looked nowhere in particular, and savoured the name out loud.

'D a m o n   R i c h .'

No-nonsense-Fran was quick to take that as a yes.

'I'll put him through.'

'Damo. You can't be calling to tell me you're going to retire … that's the everyday mindset in your one-man cop-shop in the sticks. You pounced on that when it came up, didn't you? What's that place called again?'

'Cavendish ... and don't knock it. From what Fran's just been telling me, it sounds like you get pretty close to having had enough these days. You'd be doing yourself a favour, you

know ... although you'll have to wait for me to drop off the perch first.'

'You reckon it's that good? Remind me where Cavendish is again.'

'Southern Grampians. The station's literally on the banks of the Wannon River.'

'Is that anywhere near Dunkeld?'

'We're the next town downstream. It's kinda the opposite of Dunkeld, though. Low key and non-touristy.'

'Oh yeah? Me and Wendy ventured to Dunkeld for a weekend away, just to have a feed at the Royal Mail Hotel. It lived up to the hype. Ya got a pub in Cavendish?'

'Yeah ... although it was touch and go at one stage. Before I lobbed here, it was under threat until some local cockies formed a syndicate and bought it. The latest operator they've got in the joint has made it one of the best-kept secrets on the foody trail. Actually, the whole town operates under the radar, and they seem to like it that way. Apart from every couple of years when they decide to hold the Red Gum Festival ... global pandemics permitting. They even have their own mountain, which no one's heard of. Mount Cavendish. I think it's an extinct volcano.'

'Pleased to hear you've discovered old-cop utopia, but I think I'd miss Melbourne coffee too much. So ... if you're not retiring, what can I do for you, Damo?'

'It's what I can do for you, Richard. I might have a body for you?'

'Might? You'd better explain.'

'There's a gemstone site in some bush near here. One of the fossickers has dug up or, rather exposed, some human bones. He stopped digging when he came across the feet ... presuming the rest of the body will follow. I've taped the area off.'

'And ... What do you make of it?'

'Well, that's the thing. I've got no idea. I couldn't get a look at it firsthand. Most of the fossickers don't dig too deep, but this bloke went down in a big way. Sorry Richard, but I couldn't even stand close to that hole, let alone go down it. Not with the claustrophobia thing I've got now ... Sorry,'

It sounded like he needed to catch his breath before going on.

'Being locked in that sealed food truck tomb for days ... it might seem like light years ago now, but that hasn't left me, Richard. I know you understand. You saw what that was like ... what it did to me before anyone found me. That's why I phoned you direct. I didn't want you seeing a report come across your desk and think I wasn't up to any of this.'

They listened to each other's silence until Bourke responded.

'That's fine, Damo. Don't apologise. I'm pleased you called me. None of that's relevant as far as I'm concerned. Okay?'

'Okay. Thanks, Richard.'

It was enough. Both knew the other was not desirous for more to be said on the matter. Bourke moved things on.

'So, tell me, Damo. From what the fossicker told you, do you have any idea at all whether we're talking archaeological or modern-day?'

'Sorry, mate.'

'That's okay, Damo. That's okay. I'll send Rory James. On paper, he does cold cases, but if it's present-day stuff, he can look after that too. Is there somewhere local he can stay?'

Not in Cavendish, unless he brings a caravan. He'll need to book into somewhere at Dunkeld or Hamilton. Also, there's one other thing you might want to take on board. If it turns out to be archaeological, it'll become an Indigenous matter, so I think you should have a cultural awareness presence from the get-go. Someone local if you can.'

'I'll get onto that. And this bushland … are we talking in the Grampians?'

'It's part of the bush surrounding the Grampians, on the western side. It's managed by Parks Victoria. I'll give them a heads-up if you like.'

'As thorough as ever. Anything else?'

'Yeah. There is one more thing. You can *get a good coffee in Cavendish.'*

Rory was looking at something like a four-hour drive from Melbourne to the western foothills of the Grampians. He was a good hour or more beyond Ballarat on the Glenelg Highway when Bourke phoned. Distant glimpses of the Grampians had begun to pop in and out of view.

'Where are you?' Bourke asked.

'The last place I drove through was Wickliffe. A pub and a CFA shed. But you can spot the Grampians from here. I'm booked into the Royal Mail Hotel at Dunkeld … right next to Mount Sturgeon. Their restaurant's got three chefs' hats.'

'*I know about the Royal Mail,*' he said dismissively, '*... but how far have you got to go?*'

Rory knew Bourke was well acquainted with the small-town pub that boasted an Australian top-ten epicurean reputation. He had hoped to elicit a spirited lament of envy from Bourke. Now that that hadn't happened, he was worried.

'ETA about forty minutes, I reckon. Why?'

'*Good. I need you to take a detour before you get there. Parks Victoria has come up with a local cultural heritage specialist they speak highly of. They can spare her for as long as it takes if we pick up the accommodation tab. The tricky bit is, they can't do a vehicle. You're going to have to pick her up today. Some place near Halls Gap.*'

'You're joking. Halls Gap is way up the other end of the mountains. I've been driving for over three hours as it is. Can't I do that in the morning? It's not like those feet bones are going to walk off into the bush.'

'*Sorry, Rory, it's been arranged. She's at some kind of do over there. She already passed up whatever ride home she had organised, just so you could pick her up on your way. Her boss at Parks told me she's pretty keen to arrive at the site when you do. I'll text her name and the pickup address to you. I'm sure you two can work things out from there.*'

'Why does it matter to her if I get there before she does? Doesn't she trust us?' Rory asked.

'*Didn't say. You'll have to ask her yourself. And remember, until you make the call, this is a police matter. You can take advice, but we own it until we decide we don't own it. Just don't fuck that up.'*

Fuck, Rory thought.

A text message soon arrived from Bourke. Rory pulled into a roadside parking area as he crested the next hill, then set about downloading the address and checking the map. There was no sign designating the hilltop as an official roadside stop, but it was well worthy of the label. For the first time on the drive, the Grampians filled the entire horizon ahead. A jagged blue range stretched from the looming Mount Sturgeon at their southernmost tip to the far-flung and far more imposing Major Mitchell plateau — named after the explorer and Spanish war veteran. Mitchell, the first white man to stumble across "these extreme summits of the southern hemisphere", proudly made them a mountain namesake from his native Scotland.

The Grampians' abrupt rise from the golden plain matched the legendary landscape painting, Land of the Golden Fleece, by Arthur Streeton. Rory's vantage point, a bit further south from that of Streeton, offered a self-evident view of why the Major dubbed the lengthy intervening range the Serra — Spanish for saw-toothed. Less inspiringly, it revealed too patently, just how near Rory's destination was and how far his unexpected detour would take him from a beer he could almost taste.

'Fuck'. This time he said it out loud.

The detour north ran roughly parallel to the Grampians while inching ever nearer. Their hazy blueness gradually sharpened into dramatic rockfaces until the late afternoon sun fell behind peaks. The inclines immediately transformed into silhouettes that continued to track the desolate one-car-width strip of bitumen at a safe distance. Traffic reappeared when he reached Moyston township on the main route from Melbourne to Halls Gap, the capital of the Grampians. Moyston was yet to bounce back from whatever better days it knew. Probably when it was in the throes of becoming the original home of Australian rules — "Birthplace of Australian Football" the town entrance sign proclaimed. The boast brought an ironic smile when Rory passed the Moyston cricket ground. This MCG's tree-ringed patch of motley green could be no more extreme from its Melbourne mega-stadium namesake, the *modern-day* home of Australian football.

The township also marked his arrival into the Grampians zone with a cluster of brown tourist-spot fingerboards and the odd accommodation sandwich board plonked by the roadside. The sat-nav re-awoke to tell him his destination, Grampians Pioneer Cottages, was twenty-two kilometres further along at Pomonal.

Pomonal was a different kettle of fish. The village nestled precisely where grasslands met the foot of Mount William Range. Its wooded slopes appeared to rise from the back fences of roadside paddocks, enviably gazed upon from the scattered houses. A modernist-inspired community hall told Rory he might be at the arty neck of the Grampians woods. The hall, school, general store and phone box were pretty much it at the village crossroads, but the indispensable penchants of modern travellers sprouted in surrounding paddocks and bush. Signboards heralded wineries, a cidery, olive producer, brewery, café, woolshed bistro, expansive accommodation set-ups and the ambitious proposed Wildlife Art Museum of Australia. From ancient holiday memories, Rory knew that de rigueur tourist trappings of such size were unrealisable in the mountain confines of Halls Gap. Nonetheless, they were vital adjuncts, and just kilometres down the road.

He was through Pomonal when a Grampians Pioneer Cottages fingerboard popped up to direct him onto a dirt road for his final two kilometres — not the owners sandwich board but an official road sign. This was not going to be some small affair.

Encroaching twilight signalled how knackered and hungry he now felt. His mood lightened even less when the Mazda ahead of him produced a permanent cloud of dust that could only have been escaped by reversing back to the highway. The dust didn't settle so much as thin slightly when the Mazda stopped at the property gate. A banner tied to the fence informed Rory he had arrived at the "Folk for Refugees" music event. A woman with short grey hair peeking below a slouchy knitted beret approached the Mazda. She stooped at the driver's window and delved into a bum bag to conduct entry business. As she moved on to Rory, he buzzed his window down and read her tee-shirt, "Rural Australians for Refugees, Grampians Gariwerd". This was his first reminder of the Aboriginal name for the Grampians. Gariwerd hadn't stuck as well as Uluru did for Ayers Rock, but well enough for Rory to recognise it.

'Do you have a ticket?' she smiled.

'Sorry. I'm not here for the music. I'm here to pick up …'

He hadn't expected to be having this conversation while he was in the car, let alone at a checkpoint, of sorts. He had to search his phone for Bourke's message and its attachment. Two more cars arrived behind him. He was quick about it but felt the pressure.

'… Tahlia Lock.'

'Tah? Are you sure she wants to leave now? The bands are only getting started.'

Her face knotted with concern. Rory marvelled at Tahlia being shortened to Tah.

'Um, that's what I've been told. I didn't speak to her myself, but …'

He left the sentence unfinished, deciding he didn't want to justify himself, nor play the cop card.

The gatekeeper un-stooped to scan the cars behind Rory and decided she had more pressing concerns. She re-stooped to tell him.

'I'm a bit tied down here. You'll have to go and find her yourself if you don't mind. Sorry. Just follow that last car to the carpark paddock.'

Rory felt overly trusted.

'Thanks,' he offered.

She was off to the next vehicle before he realised he didn't know what Tahlia looked like or where he might find her. Too late for that conversation.

The half-electric, half-acoustic sound of an indie band floated into the carpark paddock. People making their way from the carpark to the music were decidedly young and alternative. Rory became conscious of his work clobber. Tie-free but nudging the tie-wearing threshold … and car crumpled. The main crowd was close enough for him to notice a few puffy-jacket wearers, so he retrieved his own from the car's rear seat. As integrated as he could be, he made his way to the sizable throng, relieved to see the alternatives had brought their parents, as well as the odd grand-parent and kids. Attire stretched in a homogenous way from Fitzroy-vintage to Brighton roughing-it garb. The dress savvy might also spot more than a handful of dressed-down professionals among the local community of like-minded souls. Rory put such a harmonious gathering down to the uniting factor of its benefit cause. Still, a wider, shared ethos also seemed at play.

The beer tent wove its magic. The smell, the "psst" of cans being opened, and the vanquished prospect of waiting until he reached Dunkeld.

The bloke selling beers looked straight off the tractor, and somehow, he too fitted in. Rory decided he was a safe enough bet to ask.

'Do you know Tahlia Lock?'

'Tah? Yeah. There she is.'

He pointed to the stage.

Rory turned to the stage for the first time. He was no pisshead, but after four hours on the road, the beer tent had blinkered him to all else. He found himself watching a charismatic blond surfer dude singing as soulfully as a Teskey

Brother. The bloke accompanying him on guitar had a technique of simultaneously tapping his instrument in time, making him sound more like a whole rhythm section. Two female singers joined the choruses, one on either side of the stage. The one on the right was blonde, of about thirty years, and held a trumpet. The singer on the left was obviously Aboriginal, possibly but not certainly of full blood. She looked not much older than sixteen and probably shorter than most sixteen-year-olds, five two tops.

What the fuck? No way was this an Aboriginal cultural liaison officer — not in Rory's mind. At best, she was the work experience version, an oxymoron concept in a field many believed to be the sole domain of elders. If ever a discipline was un-work-experience-able, imparting cultural heritage had to be it.

If Rory had been sold a pup, then at least the music was good. The crowd moved closer as the singer whipped out a harmonica mid-song and led the combo into an improvised groove. Tahlia underpinned the rhythm with Aboriginal clap sticks while the harmonica, guitar and trumpet pushed the song's envelope in turn, then ramped it into the music stratosphere with echoed instrumental responses to each other. The crowd were witnessing something special, and they knew it. Spontaneous applause broke out when they finally stepped back to the vocal mics and the safer ground of choruses. The number ended, and they left the stage without the demanded encore — incapable of topping themselves.

Rory stayed by the beer tent and watched people gush praise to Tahlia beside the stage. The beer and the music had drained urgency from him, and he was happy not to interrupt … not yet. Nor did doubts about her aptness for the job manifest into worry. As far as he was concerned, there was no reason why she couldn't tag along. Finding something to eat took over as his priority.

At the food tent, he was mid-read through the blackboard list of options when he felt a tap on the shoulder. He turned to meet Tahlia's face. A much more serious face than he had seen on stage and perhaps a tad older at closer quarters. At a stretch, early twenties, he recalibrated in his head.

'Are you Rory?'

'Yes, I am.'

Rory had already thought about what he might say when he approached Tahlia, but with the shoe on the other foot, he found himself unexpectedly wordless. Tahlia extended the void with an unabashed hands-on-hips, drawn-out appraisal of what stood before her. A puzzled but not disconcerted Rory waited out the extended silent scrutiny until she arrived at a conclusion in her head.

'Okay,' she said, beamed a smile and held out her hand. 'Tahlia Lock. Pleased to meet you, Detective Sergeant.'

The smile allowed Rory to park his puzzlement.

'You, too. And you were brilliant if you haven't already been told.'

'Oh yeah, they're a great band. But I'm not a member. I was only sitting in on the chorus. I can't take any credit for their sound. But I love them, and I'm lucky they let me do that. So, how do you want to play this?'

She had moved on rapidly to preclude him challenging her modesty. It failed.

'I think they're lucky too. You added *something*.'

She smiled appreciation before he, too, moved things along.

'As for "what now", I'm here to pick you up, and I'm booked into the Royal Mail at Dunkeld tonight. I reckon that's over an hour's driving. I'm not worried how late we get there, as long as I can get a feed here before we head off. I'll phone them to make sure they've got another room available.'

Tahlia bit her lower lip. It wasn't the right answer.

'I was kinda hoping you could stay here and we could get going first thing in the morning. I didn't know you were staying at Dunkeld.'

She watched Rory's face cringe with dilemma as she spoke. She changed to sell mode.

'I can get you into one of the cottages here for the night. I know Cori. There's no way you want to drive to Dunkeld now that it's dark. It's 'roo country all the way … and you can stay on the beer,' she added, flicking her eyes to the can in his hand.

Rory blew out an exaggerated breath and swung his head to take in his surroundings. *Fair enough, she wanted to stay. Blind Freddie could see this was a big deal for her.* But he also had an agenda. That involved having already invited Michelle Fox-Jones to spend the night with him at the Royal Mail Hotel. It was the ultimate Grampians accommodation stay, and he'd managed to secure a room on his Police expenses. It was early days with Michelle — a relationship not yet sealed with a weekend away. She was unable to drop everything and be there that night but did call back to say she could swing things to come tomorrow. Her phone call locked Rory's focus onto getting to the Royal Mail Hotel no matter what. The fact that he now had a day up his sleeve added anxiety — all the more time for Michelle's willingness to evaporate … again.

He groaned.

'Cori won't charge you for sleeping here … and there's plenty more music to come. I can tell you like it.'

'How come this is sounding more like a conversation with my daughter than a work discussion?'

Rory made the observation with unintended censure, but it stung Tahlia. Her enthusing instantly gave way to clinical professionalism.

'I'm sorry, Detective Sergeant. What would *you* like to do?'

It put him even more off guard than feeling like he was arguing with his daughter Steph. He paused to make a point of appearing to ponder, then took a second pause to actually ponder. He didn't know her or anything about her yet, but she had a point … and he had to accept any rendezvous with Michelle was a day away. He looked at the beer in his hand and acknowledged he had already switched off for the day. The thought of firing up again for a night drive through mountain forests — the time kangaroos went on the move — decided it.

'Okay, you sort out the cottage, and we stay the night. I'll let the Royal Mail know we can't make it until tomorrow night.'

She smiled but not too smugly.

'Thank you, Detective Sergeant.'

'Let's stick with Rory. Okay?'

It was the last they spoke that night. Rory lasted two more beers and a few numbers by a local outfit, the Recalcitrants. When his head hit the pillow, even the sound of Orange Whip piercing the cottage walls with their frenzied take on Stax soul couldn't keep him awake.

Rory downed the cottage's toast before taking his bag to the car. Tahlia was already there, leaning on the sedan and thumbing her phone. She wore a Parks Victoria uniform and had a packed backpack and swag at her feet. The khaki shirt looked a size too big and had its sleeves rolled up to the elbow.

'You look like you need a proper coffee,' she greeted him.

'More than you know.'

'Good, we'll go through Halls Gap. I need a cooked brekky after last night. We can be there in ten, tops.'

Hall's Gap, a breach between mountain ranges, formed a portal to the inner Grampians. "*A wild romantic glen*" as its initial squatter, Charles Browning Hall, described it in the 1840s. As they approached, surrounding farmland suddenly shifted to taller mountain trees, bracken undergrowth and looming cliff faces that preserved Hall's evocative image through 150 years of evolving tourism. Fewer old-school guest houses survived these days but no less of the mountain-retreat vibe.

Both had the cooked breakfast, with a double shot long black for Rory and tea for Tahlia. They sat on the front veranda of a cute off-street house turned provedore café. Although the feed was all free-range, sourdough and charcuterie, both hangovers would have been happy with anything greasy. The coffee was tasty but lacked the fierceness of Rory's regular Melbourne dose. He ordered a second, just to be sure, and grabbed sandwiches for their lunch.

They were both sticking to small chit-chat until the main trip was underway. Even then, it had to wait until they scaled the hairpin-corner-laden drive over the Wonderland Range. Bracken fern and lichen-clad excavated-rock faces were a constant on the upper-slope side of the road. The downward side offered random killer views, like the entire Elephant Hide mountainside. Even a snail-paced caravan ahead of them couldn't spoil it for Rory.

They left the caravan to it when Tahlia directed Rory onto a gravel road descent to the Glenelg River valley. Stones clattered the sedan's low undercarriage, and before long, they were fording creek causeway crossings.

'You could have warned me.'

'Don't worry, it's the end of the season. There won't be any creeks too deep for this thing. We save a shitload of time this way by following the Glenelg River through Victoria Gap. We'll be clear of the mountains and on the Henty Highway before you know it.'

'Does that mean we don't go through Cavendish?'

'Totally. That's way off course. This is much quicker … and specky-er.'

When his head turned to her, she clarified.

'Spectacular.'

'I know what specky means. It's just that I'll need to phone Damon Rich, the local senior constable, and tell him to meet us at the site.'

'You'll have to wait. You won't get a mobile signal around here.'

'Uh-huh.'

The dirt road soon flattened and straightened out a bit. They were not in cruise-control country just yet, but the demands of driving had settled down enough for the conversation they needed to have … at least that's what the passenger decided.

'You seemed surprised when you met me last night. Am I younger than you expected?'

He took his eyes off the road to read her face. No clues there but he was reminded just how young she looked.

'I didn't know what to expect, to be honest,' he said without being entirely honest. '… an Aboriginal cultural officer is new territory for me. How does that work?'

Tahlia glanced a doubting look sideways. Rory kept his eyes on the road.

'I got this gig because I'm a qualified archaeologist. If the bones do turn out to be ancient remains, gurus from the local Aboriginal mob will be brought in after my assessment. In the meantime, I'm it.'

'Umm …'

'What?'

'A qualified archaeologist?'

'Do you want me to produce my bachelor and master's degree certificates? I can bring them up on my phone if you like.'

'Ouch.'

'Well, what did you expect?'

'If I think about it now, I wasn't surprised to see the park ranger uniform, but a qualified archaeologist in a park ranger uniform … not a concept I imagined or have come across before.'

Tahlia didn't rate the excuse, certainly not enough to spell things out any more than she needed to.

'This is a Parks Victoria uniform, not a park ranger uniform, not always the same thing. I'm sure you could have figured that much out. I've been stationed here for a while now, but my work is project-based, and I could end up in other parts of the state. What else do you want to know?'

He gave a driver's sideways glance and met her challenging glare.

'Okay. If we're getting judgemental. Last night when we met, you held back for more than a moment. You didn't exactly disguise you were weighing me up in your mind. What was going on there?'

She lifted her head to look at nothing and give thought to how she would answer.

'Um … I'm not sure how to say this because it's something someone like you doesn't have to face …'

He opened his mouth to question "someone like you" but thought better of it. Tahlia noticed and realised she'd already stepped beyond being tactful. She dived in.

'I'm young … female … and Aboriginal … and the way they set this thing up boiled down to me agreeing to spend time driving around in the middle of nowhere like this, on my own, with a male homicide cop I've never laid eyes on. Who knows what you mighta turned out to be? And before you tell me I'm over-reacting, where I grew up, being with a cop didn't always translate to being safe, usually the opposite. A kid from one school I went to, died in custody … it happened before my time there, but it happened. So, I promised myself, if I had any doubts when I clapped eyes on you, I'd make the call there and then, before anyone got their nose outta joint. Sorry, it might sound very unprofessional of me, but that's my reality.'

Rory turned his head to see her looking out the passenger window. She'd said what she had to say. Rory listened to the crunch of wheels on gravel for a good half kilometre. She was here, he reminded himself, so he'd obviously passed the audition. But still, he cogitated on the brink of simmering. Should he resent being auditioned just for doing his job? Having deaths in custody of all things thrown at him. On the other hand, she did make a valid point … or two. He didn't know where to start or where to take it. His only conclusion: *this is a Pandora's box, too dangerous to open.* He shifted to a question she had left hanging …

'So, you're not from around here. Not part of the Jardwadjali mob?'

Jardwadjali people were the original inhabitants in this part of the Grampians. Rory had done that bit of homework and decided now would be a good time to intimate he was not completely ignorant on the subject. It passed unacknowledged by Tahlia.

'Northern New South Wales. Up Murwillumbah way. My ancestors were Bundjalung people. I moved to Victoria to do archaeology at La Trobe uni in Bundoora. Now I work down here as well. I'm almost a Victorian now.'

'And your family's still up there?'

'Kinda,' she sighed, making it clear that was all she had to say on the matter.

Corrugations in the gravel road added another full stop to the conversation. The car shuddered irrepressibly whether Rory slowed or sped up. It was not until they reached a sandier section of road, a couple of kilometres further along, that talking could resume.

'Fair enough about giving me the once over,' Rory resumed, seemingly out of the blue.

Tahlia turned to give a half-smile of acknowledgement. Discussing it further had been shaken from her … if not from Rory. He pressed on.

'So, what did your radar tell you about me?' he persisted.

Don't push it, she wanted to tell him.

'I'm here, aren't I?'

The dirt road thrum returned all the way to the causeway crossing of the Glenelg River. They faced a 100-metre plus stretch of water from which pairs of white marker posts protruded at intervals to define the submerged roadway. Either side of the watery throughway was thick with marshy scrub.

'Is this what you meant by "Specky-er"?'

'It's not deep. You can see bits of the road protruding here and there.'

'*I* can't.'

'The road would be closed if it wasn't safe.'

'That might be right for four-wheel drives, but …'

'Trust me,' she replied, running out of arguments.

Rory continued to hesitate. Tahlia resorted to martyrdom.

'Do you want me to take my shoes off and wade through it for you?'

It did the trick. Rory put the sedan into drive and edged into the water.

'What I want from you is to put that in writing, so it's on your head when they send out a chopper to find us or the car, or both.'

As he said it, the wheels detached from anything firm below the surface. The car shifted to the right. Tahlia heard Rory intuitively back off the accelerator.

'Keep it going!' she yelled before he could panic and before the car had left the actual line of the underwater road. Just as quickly, the wheels grabbed something firm, and they were back on track.

'Fucking hell.'

'We'll be right now. The deepest channel is that first bit.'

'We'll be right when we reach the other side. We were floating back there.'

'Like, for two seconds. Jesus.'

Rory concentrated too grimly on navigating through the marker posts to shake his head in exasperation. When the car crawled from the shallows on the other side, Rory stopped in the middle of the dry road and got out. Tahlia followed. He gestured his arm wordlessly to where they had just emerged and began to laugh.

'I'm already gonna be in the shit when I take this car back to the pool. Imagine if it did get swept downstream, let alone what could have happened to us.'

'Stop making such a mountain out of it. You'll be back on the bitumen in ten.'

And they were. They were on the forest-lined Henty Highway looking back at the Grampians from the west. This time they tracked the grandeur of the Victoria Range, south from its northernmost point until they reached open country. Then they took a minor road signposted to Balmoral.

'You know, this is not actually part of the Grampians?' Tahlia said as they took a second turn — this time onto a bush track signposted Beear State Forest.

'Some locals call this ridge of scrub the Little Black Range because it connects with the Black Range, which is itself a little Grampians. But below the surface, this country is way older and different. Maybe that's how come it managed to spawn a gemstone site. Anthropologists wrongly labelled it Bunganditj country instead of Jardwadjali … until a modern-day researcher set the record straight in 1990.' she added.

'But not your mob in either case,' Rory heard himself say before he could stop the words leaving his lips.

'More than yours though, by a good 40,000 years.'

Chapter 3

The diggings were a moonscape of upturned soil no bigger than several suburban house allotments. Abutting two sides of the actual diggings was a semi-treed area with the well-worn appearance of having often been camped upon. It sloped to what the map called Anderson's Creek — its bed, a series of random puddles. The only permanent man-made item on site was a two-stall long-drop toilet. The door facing the diggings bore the original notice of regulations applicable to the gemstone reserve proclaimed in 1987 by the late premier, but then the Minister for Conservation Forests and Lands, Joan Kirner.

It looked like the bureaucrats had taken the piss. If it wasn't ill disposed enough having her decree nailed to the dunny door, the very first regulation they accorded to Joan was a ban on anyone remaining in the reserve who "offended against decency as regards dress". Quite possibly, this remote piece of bush could be the only place in the entire state where the government chose to impose a dress code. Considering Terry's clobber du jour, the line not to be crossed could hardly be thinner. The wider gemstone reserve was ringed with uninviting stringybark scrub, fading to grey with the approach of summer. On the final kilometres of their drive, Tahlia had informed Rory that grasses and other ground level greenery were drying ever earlier each year as climate change bit harder.

With the site to himself, Terry had set up his small caravan and awning on the perimeter of the actual diggings. His ground fire was partially contained with a couple of sheets of corrugated iron standing on their ends. Their tops were tapered and lashed together with fencing wire to fashion a chimney of sorts. About thirty metres of electrical cable ran from the caravan to a portable generator parked at the base of a tree. It was not running. Food in containers and camping cutlery and crockery for two crowded the table under the awning. There were also two elaborate folding camp chairs. Neither Terry nor his hitherto unmentioned companion were in sight.

Terry's workings in the upper portion of the diggings were circled by the crime-scene tape that Damon Rich had strung from a tree and several steel pickets driven into the ground. A hand-made, hand-operated windlass of rough-cut bush timbers spanned the pit mouth. The amount of rope on the barrel of the windlass and the surrounding piles of fresh clay confirmed this was no shallow affair.

'Are you the other cops?'

Terry's head had risen above ground level from the shaft. His and Rory's first encounter was from the wrong sides of the police tape. Rory answered with:

'What the fuck do you think you're doing in there?'

Rory's annoyance failed to register with its target.

'Finding this beauty. Check it out,' Terry enthused with glee.

Rory had asked the perfect question to launch Terry's theatrical display of his prized new thunderegg. Tahlia and Rory's impromptu induction into the world of smoky quartz crystals ensued. When that unplanned interlude began to wane, the reason for their visit could wait no longer. As Rory put it:

'Okay. Show me the body.'

Terry lifted the police tape for Rory and Tahlia to pass under. Rory baulked at Terry, still acting like he owned the digging.

'Don't push it. I could already do you for entering a crime scene. After this inspection, I only want to see you outside this tape unless I say. Letting yourself or anyone in or out of here is not your call.'

The hum of a vehicle motor forestalled Terry's response and Rory's entry under the police tape. They watched a police SUV come to a halt. Its trailing dust cloud continued past onto the diggings. Senior Constable Damon Rich alighted.

He wore the short-sleeved version of the epauleted police shirt and the baseball cap edged with a blue and white check. The most overt paraphernalia was the black pistol grip on his right thigh. His age, obviously over sixty, told of an officer winding down his career in countryside quiet. A career of having seen and done it all effused from every nonchalant stride towards the shaft.

He delivered a perfunctory 'G'day' to Terry before introductions to Rory and Tahlia.

'Have you been down yet?' Damon asked Rory.

'About to.'

'Have you actually seen the hole then?'

'Same. We're gonna do that right now.'

'Good. I haven't missed anything.'

Rory couldn't fail to sense an impending snag and Damon made sure of it with a shit-eating grin. Rory looked to Terry and nodded towards the hole.

The rectangular opening looked to be a bit less than two metres by a metre and a half. It was crowded on three-and-a-bit sides with piles of the excavated earth. Access around the lip consisted of just enough walking space to operate the windlass. The top rung of a ladder was visible above ground level on the fourth side.

Terry skipped to the far side, allowing space for the other three to gather around the hole. Rory inched to one side and rapidly gripped the windlass with both hands. Tahlia took the other side and casually rested one hand on the windlass in order to lean out over the hole and peer down.

Damon hung back. 'I'll leave that to you.'

Rory looked up to clock Damon's still-grinning face. Then he tried to stretch his neck to see downward.

The shafts' sides were bare earth entirely free of shoring timber. The ladder was an extension ladder at full stretch. It stood on a narrow platform of timber boards, invisibly secured to the mid-shaft walls. A second ladder descended from the platform to the depths beyond.

'Fucking hell,' Rory said.

'Wow,' Tahlia countered.

'How far does it go below that platform?' Rory asked.

'Bottom of the second ladder. Can't you see? Where those buckets are.'

'Oh yeah,' said Tahlia.

Rory tested the firmness of the windlass and extended his grip in order to lean further, as well as trying to stretch his neck. His eyes adjusted enough to the gloom to discern the full depth. The floor of the hole was crowded with buckets of earth ready to be hauled up.

'Where are the bones?'

'They're in the tunnel. It heads to the left from the bottom of the shaft. It goes in about three metres.'

'Fucking hell. You've got a tunnel down there as well as this fucking great hole?'

'These diggings have been worked for decades. You have to go deep for anything good, and when you do hit a seam, you go where it goes.'

'Deep's one thing. This is insane. How safe is it without any shoring? Is the tunnel protected?'

'No need. It's all clay. It's as firm as.'

Rory turned to Damon.

'I can see why you gave this a miss.'

'You wouldn't get me down there for quids.'

It was no casual remark. He had stopped grinning to say it like he meant it.

'Well, one of you has to go down,' Terry said. 'I done the right thing phoning it in. Now I need the body outta my way so I can get on with the job. I've only got one more week off work.'

'What do you mean, you "Done the right thing". And what do you mean, "body"? I thought we were talking about a few bones.'

'I've been working the tunnel a bit more while you took your time getting here. It looks like we've got a whole body's worth of bones, which …' he stressed with a pause before answering the first part of Rory's question, '… I could have simply ignored and left it down there. No one would ever come across the body again once I fill this hole in. Not now that it's become *old* ground.'

'Why would you go to all the trouble of filling it in?' Rory asked.

'That's the rule on the dunny door over there. All holes have to be filled in when you finish. That's why I've got to make the most of it while I've got a hole this deep. There have been plenty of holes this deep in these diggings, but they're all filled in.' He glanced from Damon to Tahlia and then to Rory and added, 'So, who's it gonna be?'

Rory looked at Damon to work out a police response.

'Don't look at me. It's not something I can do anymore.'

Rory understood that was that. There was a story there, but he couldn't go there.

'How safe do you reckon it is?' he asked Damon instead.

'I've never heard of one of these things collapsing, but I've only been stationed in the area for eighteen months. Even so, I wouldn't blame you if you didn't want to go down … and you don't have to when it's all said and done. You could have it assessed first … which you probably should do anyway. The union would insist on it if you asked them.'

'If you want my professional opinion …' Tahlia offered and proceeded to give it in any case. '… I think you're both being total wusses. I've been on enough archaeological sites to know this has been dug in stable clay.'

Rory peered into the hole again.

Terry could smell the doubt. As the person with the most at stake, he upped the ante.

'If you want this assessed, they'll send in some mining consultant which you won't get out of for under ten grand. You'll wait a month or more for a piece of paper that covers their arse in steel plate. They'll tell you you'll have to install some kind of re-useable shoring-panel system. The only ones you can lay your hands on quickly enough will be somewhere like Western Australia or Papua New Guinea. And you can kiss goodbye to another forty grand to get them here with a professional team of specialist installers … if you can find someone who can be bothered with such a small, out of the way job. Maybe your forensics will also want a safe space excavated and lined down there so they can examine the site. Who knows what decade you'll be in by then? On top of all that, you'll need to pay plant-hire on crane systems, a lighting rig, air circulators … you name it. But, at the end of the day, it's your call.'

Rory's face became a fixed frown.

'What if I do go down there. I won't be able to do anything. We'll still have to have the body retrieved by someone. And what state are these bones in? What can you tell us about what you've uncovered so far?'

'I'm no expert ….' Terry said, turning to Tahlia. '… but what's the period after stone-age?'

'Bronze age.'

'No. After that'

'Iron Age?'

'No. I was thinking more plastic age.'

'What the fuck are you talking about?' Rory said.

'It's a body wrapped in a blue poly tarp. When I phoned it in, all I could see was the feet bones poking out one end. No sign of a tarp.'

Rory and Damon looked at each other. Other questions were instantly begging. The fellow police officers' first response was silently acknowledging to each other that they had a murder on their hands. Rory's mind had raced ahead to join a few dots. He ran it past Terry for confirmation.

'So, you dug down into new ground, then tunnelled sideways and unknowingly encountered the bottom of another former shaft where a body has been dumped before that other shaft was refilled?'

'I'd say that's the size of it. I thought I'd be clear of other holes at that depth. But, there you go.'

'Do you know who dug the other hole?'

'Na. There's no visitors book for a place like this, and unless a club is holding an event here, you usually have the place to yourself … maybe one or two others tops. Most of the year, the cockatoos have it to themselves.'

Rory walked away from the shaft. There was serious thought to be given, and he couldn't do that on the lip of a seemingly bottomless pit.

'I reckon Terry's right,' Damon said. 'You need to see if this can be done without all that hoo-hah. If a consultant makes a call on this, even the crack squads won't touch it until the whole place is made bombproof — so to speak.'

'I'm happy to pop down and have a squiz,' Tahlia offered.

'Nice of you to offer, but this is my case to deal with.'

'Not if the bones are Aboriginal.'

'Well, we now know that's not the case.'

'Oh yeah. I must have missed the bit where you went down the shaft and carried out a professional ethnicity assessment.'

'You know what I mean.'

'I know what you assume if that's what you mean.'

Rory looked at Damon. Damon shrugged.

'Alright,' Rory said. 'I'll go down.'

'Thank fucking God someone is,' Terry said and moved to the ladder.

'I'll go first. Wait till I'm on the second ladder before you come down. The walls of the shaft are safe, but I wouldn't like to have too much weight on that mid-shaft platform. One of us at a time should be okay, though.'

'Fucking hell, shouldn't we have hard hats.' Rory said.

39

'You can use mine. It's under the caravan canopy … in case a mining inspector ever shows up,' he added to answer the surprise on Rory's face. Terry proceeded to skip down the ladder without a hard hat.

'I'm onto the second ladder. You can come down now,' his cry came.

Rory gave a roll of his eyes to Damon and Tahlia as he positioned himself on the ladder. He descended slowly.

'Fuck,' he breathed at every second rung. He said it louder as he stepped onto Terry's makeshift platform.

As he held the top of the second ladder, falling earth began to hit his hard hat, and he fell to his knees in terror. The shower of clods ended just as quickly as it happened, to the sound of Tahlia laughing.

'I couldn't resist. It was only a handful.'

'You fucking …'

'Ha ha ha,' she continued.

He slow-stormed back up the ladder, emerged, took off the hard-hat and thrust it at Tahlia.

'Okay. You do it. And take this with you and photograph it.'

He held his phone out to Tahlia.

Damon grinned. 'I'm glad you two are enjoying yourselves.'

Tahlia went to the car, returned with a bum-bag around her waist and a head torch she mounted on the hard hat. She descended both ladders with the ease of a trapeze artist. The murmur of voices wafted up as she disappeared into the tunnel. The murmuring faded to quiet.

Rory gave it a couple of minutes and then yelled into the hole.

'Can you hear me?'

No answer came, but the murmuring resumed. Thuds and clunks of activity followed.

'Can you hear me?' Rory tried again.

'Won't be long,' Tahlia's voice drifted back after too long a break. It was akin to the extended pauses television presenters experience when they converse to each other live from studios on opposite sides of the globe.

'Just take the photos and get back up here,' Rory shouted. He resisted the urge to say "Roger".

Another extended break ensued before he heard Tahlia reply.

'Okay. Won't be long.'

More rummaging sounds followed and a faint "Bloody hell" from Terry. It prompted Rory to cautiously lean out over the hole. A half-flash of camera light emitted from the tunnel at the bottom of the shaft. Then another.

Rory retreated and waited. Faint sounds of rummaging and murmuring turned to grunting. Alarm bells sounded in Rory's head.

'I need you both to come up now,' he yelled.

The hole fell silent.

Rory had been deliberately avoiding engaging with Damon. Sending Tahlia down to photograph the scene was halfway justifiable; after all, she had been contracted as a specialist. However, the longer she and Terry faffed around, the more compromised things felt. He had allowed his investigation scene to pass into the hands of civilians. Rory knew it, and Damon knew it. He finally walked over to Damon.

'I'm gonna have to go down there.'

The only allusion of control left to Rory was to stand with his hands on his hips.

'No need, mate,' he said, lifting his sight above Rory's shoulder.

Tahlia alighted from the ladder first. More surprisingly, both Tahlia and Terry were wearing disposable examination gloves. Rory's hands fell from his hips — bereft, stunned and finally infuriated in the space of a second.

'You interfered. You actually interfered with the crime scene. You and …' He struggled for a way to describe Terry. '… and this civilian. What the fuck have you done?'

'It's okay. Terry has been mining around it, and now the whole …' Now Tahlia was searching for the right word, '… parcel … has been exposed. I dug out the last bit, and we lifted it to the bottom of the shaft. Don't worry; it was done with minimum handling. It was totally not heavy, and we did it with these gloves on.'

She held both gloved hands up, and Terry followed.

'We placed it on one of Terry's planks so you can raise it with the windlass when you're ready. I doubt there'll be any residual forensics, but I gathered all the contacting soil in a couple of buckets for you. Just in case. It's all here on your phone.' She handed Rory's phone back to him. 'And now you can also see the parcel from the top of the shaft.'

Terry spoke before Rory could react.

'And I never interfered with anything. This is my shaft, and I have a miner's right to prove it. If anyone interfered, it's this body interfering with me going about my legitimate work. And in any case, I never dug next to the body. It's just that the earth between the body and where I did dig is loose refill, so it just kept falling away. I've tried to do the right thing all along. I could have dug the whole lot before I phoned it in, you know. Or I could have just chucked the body into the bush and forgot about it. But I did phone it in upfront, and I never interfered with anything. Why would I? Jesus fucking Christ.'

Everyone had said their bit … except Damon.

'Well … are you going to thank them, or do you want me to cuff 'em both.'

'What are you going to do for amusement when you actually retire, Damon?'

'Come on, Rory. It's not such a bad result, really. I've got an incident tent I can set up to place the body in. It's going to be a good while before you can get crime scene forensics out here. They'll appreciate not having it exposed in the meantime. Want me to set it up for you?'

All eyes were on Rory, with the sun behind him.

Tahlia squinted at him from under her hard hat. Her headlamp was still switched on. Terry had a permanent squint that defied the possibility of any vision capability. Damon wore shades above his constant grin.

Rory shook his head with resignation.

'Alright, Damon. You set up the tent. Can you give him a hand, please, Tahlia? I'm gonna check out these photos before we raise the body and call in forensics. Terry, you can put the kettle on. Everyone got all that?'

The resolute response was as unexpected as it was expected. The tent was up, and a cup of tea was had before Terry began winding the windlass. The body, wrapped in a blue plastic tarp, lay on a double plank. It hung on the windlass rope like a stretcher below a rescue helicopter. Tahlia steadied the body's ascent up the shaft by following it on the ladders. Once the body was above ground level, Rory and Damon each took an end while the rope was detached. They were then able to carry it to the tent and place it onto a folding table.

Rory and Damon stood back and looked at the blue parcel loosely bound with rope. Tahlia and Terry joined them. The four stood looking down in silence, ironically like people observing a coffin about to be lowered *into* the ground. Damon spoke first.

'Whoever put this body down there didn't expect it'd ever see the light of day again.'

'It's a woman,' Tahlia announced, and not without a tone of disappointment.

Heads turned to her in enquiry.

'You couldn't pick it down below, but in this light, you can see a piece of toenail and a speck of toenail polish. See?'

As was the case when Terry first made the discovery, the feet were still the only bones protruding from blue wrapping.

'Pretty recent then,' Terry concluded.

'Toenail polish has been around for over three thousand years if that's what you mean. But if you were referring to the poly tarp and nylon rope tied around it, I reckon they would have first appeared in shops back in the sixties or seventies, something like that. If you really want to narrow it down, you can go by what flesh is left on the bone. As an archaeologist, I look exclusively at skeletal bones. I can tell you that those feet bones are years away from becoming fully skeletal. Despite what it looks like, the bits left on those bones are more flesh than dirt. Your pathologist will probably have a good idea as soon as they unwrap the thing, but my best guess is … this is a female, five-foot five-ish, died four or five years ago.'

'Bravo, Ms Silent Witness. And what d'ya reckon MO wise? Blunt instrument?' Damon mocked. Not enough for Tahlia to take offence; that was left to Rory. It annoyed him that Damon wasn't treating anything seriously.

'We're not unwrapping this. This is how it stays until forensics get here. Now let's bring up those buckets of earth and put them in here too. And Damon, Forensics won't be arriving here until tomorrow. I need you to be at the site until they show up, or have someone sent out from Hamilton. I don't want anything else happening to this body behind our back. Okay?'

Rory's words were pointed and loaded.

'Your call,' was the best face-saver Damon could offer.

'No, it's not him.'

Tahlia was on her phone and pacing beyond the bush toilets. They comprised two adjoining sit-down cubicles screened across the front and on two sides by a full-height timber plank fence. Because the seats were positioned above once-deep pits

45

in the ground, good ventilation was vital, even if it was a losing battle. That requirement had been addressed by raising the corrugated iron roof nearly half a metre above the walls, creating a gap to the outside world on all sides. No tank was installed to capture rainwater from the roof. Perhaps it was considered an unnecessary measure in the absence of flush cisterns.

'Because the body's a female,' she answered after a listening silence. Another pause ensued.

'I know what I told you, but it isn't him. I shouldn't have said anything. Alright?'

More listening.

'Don't you think I'm disappointed too? He's also my brother.'

Pause.

'It's still too early to tell. I'm still trying to figure him out. I'll let you know when I know. Okay?'

Pause.

'I know, and I'm sorry too. I'll call you when I get home. See ya.'

Tahlia ended the call and headed back to the incident tent.

Rory waited before he exited the adjoining male toilet, wondering what he'd overheard and how he was going to wash his hands.

Chapter 4

The trip to their motel in Dunkeld took Rory and Tahlia through Cavendish. The town of less than 500 souls had one of everything — one cop, one pub, one shop. Rory chose the one pub — the Bunyip Hotel.

'I need at least one drink after that.'

'Aren't you on duty?'

'Yes and no. I might pick up some useful intel from the locals,' he rationalised.

They carried schooners of beer to a table on the pub's outside deck. A grassy slope fell fifty metres to the red-gum lined Wannon River. Occasional traffic passed over the road bridge on the view upstream. The downstream view showcased the tall, disused timber railway bridge. Pubgoers sitting there prior to the nineteen-eighties would have observed Wimmera wheat trains rumble across en-route to the seaport of Portland. Rory and Tahlia were the only people sitting outside.

'Nice,' Tahlia said.

Rory's mind wasn't taking in his surroundings.

'I could arrange a ride back to Halls Gap for you if you like, now that we're back to civilisation.'

'Aren't you forgetting the job I'm here to do?'

'What? You reckon this body's gonna turn out to be Indigenous? Come on.'

'So, what are you saying? You don't want me involved now?'

'No. It's not that. I thought I'd be doing you a favour. There's nothing to suggest this is an Indigenous body or that it's culturally related in any way. I thought you thought that too, and you'd probably be wanting to get back to your life.'

'I'm here 'til it's shown that I no longer need to be.'

It was a full stop. Tahlia sat back in her chair and sipped her beer.

Rory sat back in his chair too but eschewed his beer for the moment. He gave Tahlia an overtly knowing look.

'You know what I reckon? I reckon you've got some other agenda going on here. Fucked if I know how that could even be or how it could remotely be connected, but I think you'd better be upfront with me now before you have anything more to do with this case. I'm not gonna let myself or the investigation be ambushed or compromised by some entirely unrelated affair that I know nothing about.'

'So, you *did* hear me on the phone?'

'Yeah, but not by choice.'

'Yeah, well …'

She crossed her arms, dropped her head and stared at the half schooner of beer she had placed back on the table.

'Well, are you gonna tell me what's going on?'

'Long story.' She continued to stare at the beer.

'I'm not going anywhere anytime soon. In fact, I reckon I could settle in here.'

He took in his surrounding for the first time as he said it. Tahlia placed her palms on the table and lifted her head, and drew a long breath. Rory noticed her eyes had welled.

'It's my brother. He went missing around here four years ago.'

She left it at that.

'That's not such a long story.'

She braced herself to proceed.

'He's older than me, and he came to Victoria to do archaeology at La Trobe uni like I did. After he graduated and before he got an archaeology job, he and a couple of his uni mates came to the Grampians to check out the Aboriginal rock shelters. It wasn't an official activity, but one of their tutors did consult with the traditional owners so they could also visit sites not normally accessible to tourists. The owners arranged a local Indigenous guide for their field visits.

'Anyway, my brother went missing. Not when he was visiting sites with his mates but where they were staying. They were at a hostel in Halls Gap, and one morning he wasn't there, which wasn't that unusual, but he never returned. All his travel gear was still there, including his sleeping bag. He'd gone out for the day and was never seen or heard from again.

'His mates reported him missing when they realised he wasn't coming back, but the cops hardly wanted to know. Their take was — young back packer does a runner from a hostel before he'd settled up for the room … and he's Aboriginal. There was no search organised, no media alerts. When my mother came down from Queensland, she had to battle to have him registered as a missing person. They kept telling her he'd probably just "gone walkabout". They actually said that to her. They told her: her best bet was to go back home. That was far enough away for him to dare show his face again.'

She wiped her nose on the back of her hand.

'And you have actually moved here and got a job here hoping to … I dunno. What are you hoping to achieve? I can understand you can't let something like that go, but … I can't imagine where you can go with it on your own.'

'I know,' Tahlia acknowledged quietly. 'But the Parks Victoria job came up, and I would have applied for it in any case. It wasn't even based here to begin with. The first project I worked on was in the Mallee. The Grampians stuff came later. It wasn't part of a planned obsession, but now that I'm here, I can't help trying to find out what I can.'

'And then I come along with a mysterious body in a gemstone mine …'

'It fell in my lap. I didn't want to die wondering … although it did leave me hoping and not-hoping at the same time.'

Rory let go of questioning her actions.

'Sorry. What's your brother's name?'

'Ricky.' It caught her breath to say it.

'It couldn't have been easy to even think the body could have been … Ricky. Even if it was the longest shot. After all, we were expecting archaeological remains,' Rory said.

'Mum and I have accepted that he's probably not alive, but I know that whatever happened to him happened in the Grampians. I know that because his car was found six months or so after he went missing. It was involved in a fatal crash at Warrnambool. Two young guys had stolen it. One of them was also an Aboriginal kid, so the cops weren't even convinced it was stolen. A bro doesn't steal a car from another bro.

They didn't follow through, but I tracked down the guy who survived. He admitted to me that his mate, the one killed in the crash, told him he only "sort" of stole the car. He and some other guys came across it abandoned in the bush when they were trail bike riding. The keys were in it, but the battery was dead. They came back with a car and jumper leads, and it spluttered back to life, so they just took it. When I asked him where they found it, all he'd been told was "up round Rocklands", which doesn't narrow it down much at all. That's the second largest lake in Victoria. It's surrounded by bushland on the western side of the Grampians.'

Rory thought, elbows on the table, his chin resting on his clasped hands.

'Did you tell the police about that?'

'Are you kidding?'

'But you *would* like them to know and to investigate things properly?'

'I've given up on miracles.'

'Maybe so, but you've been sizing me up from the moment we met. Has this all been one big audition? Checking me out as someone who might pick up the cudgel for you?'

Having her ulterior motive called out stung Tahlia into wrath.

'Well, what if I was? I already tried going through the front door and got told to fuck off. Big surprise that was, hey?' she blurted before winding back to mere fierce determination. 'You know, some people say there's this mythical creature called a "good-cop". Maybe I got my hopes up … I dunno what I was thinking. You've probably already dismissed the whole thing, like the rest of them. Forget it.'

She folded her arms and slumped on the chair. Rory, still in a thinking pose with his elbows on the table, tapped his clasped hands on his chin and digested the story. He arrived at a conclusion in his mind and nodded.

'I'll check it out for you. See if it's been underdone like you say. The car story sounds like it could be new evidence … or at least a lead. I'll pull up the file and see if it rates a mention. Okay?'

She remained hunched but lifted her eyes to him. 'Underdone is an understatement, but alright. That would be nice. Thank you.'

'Text me his full name, age, the date he went missing and anything else you've got. And what you know about the car — dates, the survivor's name and contact. No promises beyond that. Unless there's a body or the likelihood of a body, it's not my turf. Sorry to put it so bluntly.'

'Don't be. I *am* grateful you're not dismissing it.'

Chapter 5

Rory and Tahlia rolled into Dunkeld twenty-four hours after Rory's originally intended ETA. Dusk had fallen on the landscape but had it been midnight, there'd still be no mistaking the towering Grampians peaks coming to an abrupt halt on the town's doorstep. That earned the name Mount Abrupt for one of those peaks.

Since white settlement, the mountains had always attracted tourists to Dunkeld to a greater or lesser extent. Nonetheless, as the twentieth century drew to a close, it joined the downward spiral afflicting most small country towns across Australia. By then, the small pub was run down, the population had shrunk, and the footy club went into recess.

All that changed once the millennium ticked over … and it changed in a way that other towns could only dream about. The alleged second-ever Dunkeld-ite to go to university had evolved into a QC, successful businessman and philanthropist on the list of Australia's 100 most wealthy. Allan Myers' fondness for his hometown led to him buying the pub and having it revamped and extended by award-nominee architects from the big smoke. His vision literally extended above and beyond to have the town's unsightly powerlines placed underground and decaying homes torn down to open up street views of the mountains.

Most legendary, Myers' Royal Mail pub went on to become a two chefs' hat, Australian Restaurant of the Year. On any given weekend, you're battling foody pilgrims to get a park in the main street. Even the footy team was re-born, albeit by way of a merger with nearby Glenthompson.

'There's a room booked in your name. No need to pay anything, but they'll want your credit card details in case you hit the mini-bar,' Rory told Tahlia as they sat in the parked car.

'Thanks,' said Tahlia.

They had arrived at the Royal Mail, and Rory was feeling an obligation to look after Tahlia. Did she expect them to dine together? Could he avoid doing so in any case? If they both ended up going to the same hotel dining room, they could hardly eat at separate tables, and therein lay the root of Rory's boundless overthinking.

Michelle Fox-Jones had texted him half an hour previously. She had already arrived and registered and was waiting in her and Rory's room. Rory hadn't told Tahlia about Michelle or that he and Michelle planned to dine at the hotel. It dawned on him that with Michelle in tow, a dining room encounter with Tahlia would rank even higher on the awkwardness scale. An introduction and some glib comment perhaps to explain their presence — but nothing close to extinguishing questions left hanging in Tahlia's head. Tahlia would clearly be intending to eat in, so he would be obliged to ask her to dine with him and Michelle. What if she felt obliged to accept, not realising that this was a relationship struggling to take off and remain airborne? Rory and Michelle had well and truly transcended the having sex landmark, but this would be the first time they would spend a night together — a chilling prospect for one PTSD sufferer, let alone two. The unspoken fear each held of hysteria-inducing nightmares erupting in the presence of the other was akin to walking a high-wire. On every previous occasion they had had sex; an excuse not to "sleep-over" at the other's flat had always been proffered and always been accepted without question. At Dunkeld, the elephant in the room was: there would be no such safety net. What pressure? Two was company; three would be a crowd of MCG proportions.

'Err, about a meal tonight …'

It was far from being an actual question, but he couldn't think how to end the sentence and left it at that.

'The shop on the corner does really good pizza. I'll probably get one and take it back to my room. Hope you don't mind.'

That cleared the decks absolutely for him and Michelle to dine uninterrupted, but he wanted to come clean nevertheless. He felt sufficiently emboldened — if not excited with relief — to blurt it out:

'I have a friend staying with me tonight. We'll be eating at the hotel.'

She turned her head full on to him in the car and paused before saying.

'A female?'

Rory looked at the windscreen.

'Yes. We're …'

Again, he was unable to finish the sentence. He had not yet had reason to describe their relationship, and now that he was put on the spot, every version he came up with in his head sounded wrong. *Girlfriend. Lady friend. She's just someone I'm seeing. It's okay, I'm separated. We've only been seeing each other for a while … agh.*

'Okay. So, you're not gay. Can you pop the boot so I can get my pack out? I'll see you in the morning.'

Michelle was a former detective-sergeant Rory had known of, who, to his twofold surprise, he had become acquainted with after she quit the Force. The first surprise was that Michelle, who he knew left the job on stress, had also been diagnosed with PTSD. Unlike Rory, who had shot and killed an armed perpetrator, Michelle was not known to have been involved in any significant traumatic event. He learnt that her trauma resulted from accumulated exposure to the mandatory component of all homicides — dead bodies. Often, they were bodies that had the life beaten out of them by other humans. Tortured bodies, raped bodies, infant bodies. Her cumulative PTSD was a hitherto un-labelled phenomenon to Rory.

His second surprise: Michelle was going public about her PTSD. She was writing a book and had sought input from the

Force. They didn't exactly offer their endorsement, nor did they put up the shutters. They were sensitive about the possibility of being portrayed in an unsympathetic light, and they were also open to something that might change attitudes about PTSD for the better — probably in that order. The Force had suggested Rory's name to Michelle as a success story, someone who was sidelined for a year by a very public trauma and made a successful return to work, albeit as a one-man cold case unit. As Inspector Bourke tried to sell it to Rory, "They reckon you're a success story. You're the one that came back. Like you say, you're back on the horse, nabbing bad guys ... well, at least *a* bad guy. You're their poster boy. You're a chance for them to claim that all their new workforce improvement stuff is working and is all touchy-feely."

Rory was obligated to have a coffee with Michelle despite railing against the suggestion. He had his own good reasons to decline being written about, and he politely stuck to his guns. What he hadn't anticipated was the understanding of a fellow sufferer and how much solace that brought. Not the academic understanding of the workplace insurer's psychiatrist, but authentic, lived insight and compassion. Michelle reluctantly took "no" for an answer, but they didn't part without both dancing around the possibility of catching up again in any case. Something else was at play.

PTSD had played a part in both becoming separated from their spouses. By the time he and Michelle met, only Rory was seeing someone — the determined-to-remain-independent Sigrid Dobell. Sigrid lived in Bendigo, a taxing two-hour drive from Rory's flat near St Kilda. Before too long, Rory was saving money on petrol.

'The food will be just as amazing without the view,' Rory apologised. They had a window table in the hotel's Wicken's restaurant, but night stole the view of Mount Sturgeon's ragged cliff faces staring down upon them.

'I'm surprised they haven't flood lit the mountain. Every other detail is spot on.' Michelle replied.

They had settled on having the eight-course degustation menu matched to Australian wine. The sommelier had poured them a local Riesling and, they awaited the arrival of their first plate.

'To our first night away together,' they toasted. The significance of the milestone had never been discussed, and they were about to begin. A tacit form of mutual denial was at play, both determined for the occasion to appear normal.

'Even if the room is paid for by the Force,' Michelle added.

'Now you know I'm cheap.'

'Hardly, this meal's going to set us back … unless you're going to do a runner after we've eaten.'

'Not with a room booked and paid for.'

'So, you're planning on having dessert,' Michelle flirted.

Talk soon shifted to the case that brought Rory to Dunkeld, something he could converse easily about with a former Detective Sergeant, notwithstanding rules that forbade such sharing.

'We recovered a female body from the bottom of a gemstone mine-shaft that had been filled in. The body was wrapped in a poly tarp. Forensics will be here in the morning to unwrap it.'

'So, nothing archaeological after all? I suppose it's not even a cold case. Will Bourke keep you on it?'

'Maybe not. I'll get an idea tomorrow … so we'd better enjoy this opportunity.'

'I intend to,' she smiled as their confit hens' yolks arrived. The sommelier followed to top up their glass.

'How did you go in Ballarat?' Rory asked.

Part of the planets aligning for their Dunkeld stay was Michelle "almost" being in the neighbourhood at Ballarat. It was halfway from Melbourne but still well over an hour from Dunkeld. She had spent the day there interviewing a PTSD sufferer for her book. She shook her head in response to Rory's question.

'Good, but … he's another case of a cop battling stigmatisation as well as PTSD. Sound familiar?'

'Maybe, but isn't that what your book's about? Something that will help change the culture and attitudes.'

'Of course, it is, but it's still depressing to witness first-hand. The Force has got such a long row to hoe. Anyway, I'm telling you how to suck eggs. As depressing as today might have been, it's all grist for the mill. Like you say, it strengthens my proposition. That's the silver lining … in addition to me being here tonight,' she clarified.

Michelle's eyes betrayed her flirty smile. They reflected the same uneasy adventurism that Rory was feeling.

'To silver linings,' Rory proposed with his glass.

Rory was indeed a battler of stigmatisation as well as PTSD. Although Force command trumpeted him as the hero who halted a knife-wielding maniac in his tracks by killing him, rank and file members were of a different mind. A then-married Rory had responded to the scene because he and senior constable Heidi Lester just happened to be passing on their way to a lunchtime tryst. He fired his pistol when the knife-wielder shrugged off Heidi's capsicum spray. Rory had ignored the standing instruction to aim at the torso, mindful of his own pre-considered notion that armed cops should be able to halt life-threatening nut-jobs without having to kill them. Rory's leg-shot found its mark alright, but failed to stop the perpetrator's lunging. He shredded Heidi's outstretched arm before Rory's enraged second, third and fourth shots riddled the torso. Members of the force saw it as an entirely preventable tragedy to one of their own. Nor were they impressed that Rory needed a year off for simply doing his job. Rory's wife was equally unforgiving when the episode brought his affair to light. Separation quickly ensued, as it also did in his relationship with Heidi. PTSD seemed the least of his worries.

Chapter 6

Tahlia was waiting by Rory's unmarked car again when he emerged from his room in a detached motel-like row. He kissed Michelle goodbye, more modestly than he might have done without an audience, especially after the unspoken breakthrough-event of spending a night together without incident — other than bountiful euphoric sex. He wandered over to the car, concentrating hard not to look smug. Tahlia, dressed in her Parks Victoria garb, peered around Rory and exchanged a tiny wave with Michelle, whom she had never laid eyes upon. Michelle's return wave was tinier.

'Cosy,' she said as Rory neared and turned to place her pack in the boot.

'Michelle's working down this way, so we thought we'd catch up,' he stammered to her back. *Fuck*, he thought as he heard the words leave his lips. *How naff does that sound?*

They reached the car doors and faced each other across the roof, ready to hop in. Tahlia answered Rory's thought with an unmistakably doubting cock of the eye and a raised eyebrow.

'I do have a private life,' he shrugged.

'It looks more like a case of *what happens in Dunkeld stays in Dunkeld*, if you ask me.'

'A man and a woman in a relationship spend a night in a hotel room,' he shrugged again. 'All the same, I'd appreciate it if you didn't mention it to any of my colleagues. There are a few who would try and make something of me taking advantage of a room paid for by the Force.'

'Like I said, *what happens in Dunkeld ...*'

Rory sighed and got in the car.

Rory's phone pinged as they neared the turnoff to the gemstone site. He lifted his phone from the console to read the text message.

'Hey, you're a cop. You can't use your phone while you drive.'

Rory read the text before answering her.

'Well, it's just as well I did read it because Cockburn has shown up at the site.'

'What's Cockburn? Some weird cop STD. Anyway, I'm a woman. I don't have the wherewithal.'

'Gary Cockburn is a homicide Detective Sergeant, and believe me, you're not safe. He gets the job done when it comes to criminals, but he's at the other end of the scale from that mythical creature you referred to as a "good cop". No one or nothing is off limits with Gary, so if he baits you, whatever you do, don't bite. Bite your tongue if you have to, turn the other cheek, whatever you do, don't engage.'

Tahlia gave a dubious look.

'I mean it. He can be a piece of work. The only thing working in your favour is, I'll be there. With me around, I become his main target. Always.'

'Cockburn. Is that his real name, and what's his problem anyway?'

'His name's part of it. I heard he's copped shit about it all his life. When he was growing up, he wanted to change it, or at least pronounce it *Co-burn*. His dad wouldn't have a bar of that. And he's short.

'In my case, he blames me for one of his ex-girlfriends getting her arm disfigured. When all that transpired, she was in the Force and having an affair with me. As it so happened, it *was* my fault that her arm was disfigured.'

Rory was surprised at how easily he was confessing his own misdemeanours. Saying it out loud and so directly had always been a problem for him, even to the workplace insurer's shrink and later to Michelle.

Tahlia sensed him being overly frank. She didn't know what to say.

'Anyway. Tread carefully,' Rory added.

After a kilometre of thinking, Tahlia came up with a question.

'If Cockburn is here, does that mean he'll take over the case, and you'll be off it?'

'It could turn out that way. I'm cold cases. He's regular homicide, which is what this looks like now.'

Another silent kilometre passed.

'Don't worry, I'll still look at your brother's case.'

She gave a small smile to the windscreen.

By the time they reached the turnoff onto the dirt road into the bush, Rory and Tahlia found themselves third in a group of four vehicles. The lead vehicle was a van marked Crime Scene Investigation. The second was a marked Hyundai SUV. Dust soon had the trailing vehicles hanging back, albeit in vain as the dust stubbornly refused to settle or drift away. A large motor-home sized vehicle with impossibly low ground clearance had nosed into the first side track. It too bore a police badge and the description: Analytical Services. Rory pulled up and buzzed his window down to speak to the cop standing by the parked vehicle.

'We'll get stuck if we go any further in this. I'm gonna stay here until we know if we're needed,' she told Rory.

Even without the mobile lab, the full parade of responders was in the throes of arriving at the gemstone site. Marked police cars and vans as well as a couple of unmarked cars, an ambulance and what looked like the Government undertaker's vehicle. Two women and a bloke were erecting a larger marquee behind the tent in which they had placed the body.

Rory was surprised someone had seen fit to mention it to the media. A contingent of camera persons and reporters gathered by their own well signed vans at a required distance.

He noticed two female presenters queuing at the long-drop toilet. *Hope you brought some water to wash your hands,* he thought. As he thought it, he saw them break into a cheer at the sight of a portable toilet being towed in by the vehicle behind Rory's. Incongruously, that made the invaded-bush scene seem slightly less incongruous.

'Is that Cockburn?' Tahlia asked before they had even come to a halt.

His short, wiry, charged frame and number-one buzz-cut among a group of five or so people chatting beside the tent was unmistakeable, even to the non-familiar. Among the group was the equally wiry frame of Terry, still sporting the same pair of shorts and nothing else, and in his case, a permanently dust-filled mass of head and facial hair. Another bloke was wrestling his way into white disposable coveralls.

'What's she doing here?' Cockburn spat when Rory and Tahlia alighted and approached the group.

'I'm right here if you want it from the horse's mouth,' Tahlia shot back before Rory could answer. *So much for not biting,* he thought.

'Yeah? Well, there's nothing cultural here, or is wrapping a dead body in a poly tarp and chucking it in a hole how it's been done for the last 100,000 years?'

'No, it isn't. You can thank white men for thinking that was a good idea, let alone what they'd dream up for dealing with a black fella. I'm here until someone can prove to me that this body is non-Indigenous.'

Tahlia and Cockburn were facing each other a metre apart.

'Hey, keep it professional, Gary,' Rory interjected. '… and let me introduce you to Tahlia Lock, a cultural heritage specialist with Parks Victoria.'

'We just met; you might have noticed.' Cockburn said without shifting his glare from Tahlia.

'Yes, we have. Detective Cock-burn has been letting me know just how receptive he is to cultural heritage.'

Rory closed his eyes at Tahlia's emphasis on Cockburn. *Why did I waste my breath warning her? Now she was baiting him.*

Until then, Cockburn had merely been having his version of fun. Now Rory saw colour rise in his face.

'It's Detective Sergeant, by the way, and you know as well as I do that the chances of that body being Indigenous are a million to one.'

Tahlia upped the ante. 'Pretty good odds. So, what do you reckon? My house against your house?'

The reality of the challenge caused Cockburn to pause.

'What is this shit? Do you even own a house?'

'I could knock up a bark humpy over there if you like,' she gestured to some surrounding bush.

'Fucking hell. Have your sarky fun while you can because when we unwrap that tarp, you couldn't be more off this case.'

'Is that how long it will take you to get a DNA analysis?'

'Oh. I forgot. White fellas are the new black fellas these days, aren't they? Are you seriously going to put us through that hurdle?'

Cockburn was alluding to controversies about light-skinned people claiming Aboriginal heritage.

'I think you mean, *over* that hurdle … or maybe, *through* that hoop.'

'For fucks sake,' Cockburn responded.

Rory tried again. 'Alright, Gary. If you want to end up in a conduct hearing, then don't count on me telling a different story to what I'm witnessing right now. Tahlia's been formally engaged by the Force to do a job. Are you going to start respecting that and let it take its course … or what?'

It brought a brief lull as Cockburn computed the implications. He made a show of looking at his watch.

'Sure. Let's allow it to run its course. That'll take, what? Half an hour, tops? Anything else?'

'Yeah. What's the story with forensics?' he asked Cockburn.

Tahlia shook her head at Rory resuming normality so readily. Cockburn noticed and loaded his answer accordingly.

'They're ready to open the tarp now and make sure we're dealing with a whole body. Like I just said, it shouldn't take long at all. Then it's off to the coroner for a pathologist to do what they do. Forensics will hang around to check the area, but no one has volunteered to chase evidence down the shaft, and I don't blame them.'

Tahlia chipped in.

'I gave it a good going over when I was down there. Admittedly I had an archaeologist's look, but I had a decent light, and I was thorough. I'm happy to go down there again if they want me to go over it with any of their own gear.'

'You've been down there?' Cockburn said, sounding more impressed than he would have wanted to.

'Tahlia helped retrieve the body,' Rory said.

With that comment, any newfound respect Cockburn had for Tahlia evaporated.

'Oh. I heard about that cockup.'

'If me and Terry hadn't moved it a few metres to the windlass, that body'd still be down there, and you lot would be up here twiddling your thumbs for god knows how many more days or weeks.'

Rory had had enough.

'Fuck you two. Let's just get on with the job. Okay?'

A white plastic floor sheet covered the entire inside of the larger tent. The blue body parcel had been moved to the larger tent. It and the folding table upon which the body parcel was originally placed were shifted holus-bolus to avoid further disturbance. The protruding feet bones remained the only clue that a human body was enclosed within. A stand-mounted flood light came on to the sound of a portable generator throbbing to life at a distance.

A select team assembled around the table in their uniform of disposable white coveralls, masks, blue examination gloves and surgery caps. The team comprised the head forensic officer, a younger than middle-aged woman named Helen De Vries, her assistant Andy, Rory, Cockburn, and Tahlia.

'Let's see what we have then,' Helen said, scissors in hand. She proceeded to cut the distinctive nylon rope, blue with regular yellow flecks. It showed no deterioration from however long it had been buried at depth. She drew the rope away and handed it to Andy, then she signalled to Andy to take one end of the tarp flap. Together, they lifted it slowly in an arc until the flap draped over the table edge. It was enough to reveal the dressed body of a blondish woman.

Numerous black patches had formed on some areas of exposed and shrunken skin — on the hands, face, and bare legs. Signs of skeletonization only appeared where the feet had been directly exposed to earth. The lips had shrunk from her teeth to create an exaggerated grimace, and the body lay in a near foetal position. Shoulder-length hair with a lack of any grey suggested she had not reached middle age. The body was dressed in a whiteish woollen cardigan over a white top with a black skirt that looked neither too long nor too tight. There was no obvious sign of a cause of death.

'Well, there you have it, lady and gentlemen. A human body. Female, white but of yet to be determined ethnicity.'

The latter comment, obviously for Tahlia's benefit. It seemed word had spread.

Anything to suggest murder?' Cockburn asked.

'Nothing obvious that I can see. Matted hair on the back of her head might be from a blow. Those black patches on her neck could be from strangulation. As you can see, there are similar black patches on some of the other exposed skin. With a corpse in this state, it could be neither of those things. And I'm not going to start poking around. You'll have to wait for the pathologist.'

'Married, I see,' Rory said, pointing to rings.

'Age?' Cockburn again.

'God knows. You can judge as well as I can at this stage. Anything from thirties to fifties. Could even be younger. Don't quote me. It can be deceiving with this amount of decomposition. Wait for the pathologist.'

'Don't quote you? You didn't say anything,' Cockburn said.

'Well, look at what we're dealing with. Unravelling this is gonna take a lot of lab work.'

'And when she was buried?'

This time Helen answered with a do-I-have-to-say-it-again gesture.

'So, we're done here?' Cockburn asked.

'Pretty much. We still have to document it and photograph everything, of course, but you can leave us to get on with that.'

'Thanks,' Cockburn said and cocked his head to Rory to follow him out of the tent.

'Do you mind if I have a closer look?' Tahlia asked Helen.

Everyone other than Tahlia and Helen froze for an instant and then tried to act normal.

'Sure. But don't touch anything,' Helen answered.

Cockburn and Rory resumed their exit from the tent.

'So, we've got a live one,' Cockburn began, oblivious to the irony of his words. He continued as they came to a halt facing the shaft. 'I was chatting to Terry before you got here. He reckons whoever buried that body that far down must have thought they were home and hosed. No one would ever be dumb enough to re-dig old ground, especially that deep. It all has to be done by hand, you know. They're not allowed to use any machinery. That's probably why really deep shafts are not common, according to Terry, let alone blokes prepared to tunnel sideways. This is a body that was meant to stay buried.'

'Except these un-findable bodies do keep getting found.' Rory said. 'It's Murphy's law.'

'If it was me, I would'a taken it north and fed it to a croc. No one's gonna un-digest croc shit and piece it back together.'

'Nah, but you'd probably get copped by a random vehicle search on your drive north. That's how Murphy's law works with dead bodies … and it keeps us in business.'

'Yeah., well. They sent me here when they heard it was unlikely to be ancient history after all. So, I'll take it from here … let you run your "cultural heritage specialist" back to where she came from.'

Rory wondered if Cockburn ever heard what came out of his own mouth. How much snideness he could pack into every sentence?

'More than happy to leave you to deal with the media and take a statement from Terry, who, by the way, has got a partner in tow who has managed to remain invisible throughout this whole saga. You might also wanna ask the local detective if they know of any women gone missing in recent times.'

Tahlia arrived beside them.

'She's not Indigenous if that narrows it down for you. You should'a taken that bet,' she told Cockburn.

'Hey, I don't need either of you two telling me how to suck eggs.'

'You suck 'em however you like Gary. See you back at the office.'

Chapter 7

Rory kicked off the car conversation.

'Could you really tell she wasn't Indigenous?'

'Nah. I just said that because it's probably true, and I didn't want him gloating in my face when he found out for himself.'

'So, you figured Cockburn out pretty quickly.'

'White fragility dickheads like that … goes with the territory in my world. They can't help having a dig.'

'Cockburn can't, doesn't matter who you are.'

'Oh, I'm pleased to know you don't think he discriminates.'

'Shit. You've gotta stop giving me a hard time. You know what I meant.'

'Yeah, sorry.' She offered an apologetic half-smile. 'But how does he get away with shit like that? Doesn't he end up with HR on his back?'

'The police force is a strange beast. They boldly embrace cultural issues of the day, but someone famous once said, prejudices are "most difficult to eradicate from the heart." Cockburn's not without the odd like-minded colleague. Fortunately, most of them at least know how to behave in company. Why? Do you want to report him?'

'Nah. That's a fight I can do without.' She shifted tack. 'Are you off the case now?'

'Only if my boss says so. We'll sort that out back at the office. For now, I am happy to get away from Cockburn and leave all the due diligence stuff to him. His offer was too good to refuse.'

Tahlia nodded and sank into a car passenger reverie.

They swung left from the bush track onto the single lane of bitumen — heading east on the too-obviously named East-West Road. The Grampians' Victoria Range spanned the horizon ahead, a view venerated by Major Mitchell. "... *the pinnacle summits of the Victoria range presented an outline of the grandest character.*" A century and a half on, and nothing had changed.

As he had turned onto the sealed road, Rory noticed for the first time that the gemstone site was not signposted. Any visitors would have to have prior knowledge of its existence and whereabouts. Not a promoted tourist attraction, it appeared.

A little further on, a bloke was milling timber in a paddock at the first farm house they passed. Two kilometres beyond that, Tahlia roused from her wistful contemplation.

'I thought you would have spoken to that guy sawing timber. It's the closest house to the diggings. If anyone's going to be a local authority, isn't he your man?'

Rory turned and looked at her with incredulity, then slowed to a halt and negotiated a three-point U-turn.

They both alighted from the car to meet the timber miller. The miller lifted his head to register their arrival before continuing his run through the log. He docked the compact, rail mounted blade but left the engine running, removed his earmuffs and safety glasses and strode to meet them.

'Mack Adams,' he announced as Rory and Tahlia introduced themselves and shook hands with raised voices.

'What's going on? I saw all the cops and an ambulance driving past earlier. Has there been an accident?'

'It was no accident. Someone dug up a body at the gemstone diggings.'

'Holy ... Hang on, I'll turn that off.'

Individual saw teeth sharpened into focus as the blade ground to a halt. The imagined sawing sound lingered in the countryside silence.

'Goodness me. Do they know who?' He was old-school country, not the type to swear in front of a lady.

'No. She's been buried for a long while, so we'll have to rely on lab matches to identify her.'

'A woman. Gosh. That's not good.'

'No. I take it you know about the gemstone site.'

'Too right. My grandfather James discovered it. He lived here. This place has been in our family since his father selected it. Anyway, my grandfather was riding his horse through the Big Scrub in the 1920s — that's what they call that ridge of bush — on his way to the block we've got on the other side. When he was caught in a thunderstorm, he sheltered in the hollow of a big gum tree. After the storm, he noticed some sparkling gems had been exposed in all their glory by the rain. My grandfather kept the location of his find secret for twenty or more years, believing they would be worth something. He eventually shared his secret in the 1940s with his brother in-law on the proviso that he also kept it secret. The following week, the finding appeared in the Warrnambool Standard newspaper. Ha ha ha ha ha.'

'There's probably a moral in there somewhere,' Rory said.

'Probably.'

'Do you know if it gets many visitors?'

'Yes and no. It didn't really become popular until the 1980s … and when I say popular, I mean mainly among fossickers. You'll often find one or two camped there, but by the same token, you'll often find no one there. There's always a good roll up at Easter, but no one's keeping records or anything, so it's hard to put a figure on it. The locals all know about it, of course. You'll usually see them pop in briefly if they have visitors they're showing around the district. If you put me on the spot, I'd have to say there'd be more days without visitors at the site than days with visitors.'

'Hmm. So, if there's no record of who's visiting the place, I assume there's no record of who digs where or who dug the hole where this body was found.'

'You've got Buckley's hope. The gemstones are only found in that small area that everyone has been working for decades. There's probably been thousands digging the same holes over and over. These days, you'll only find new ground by going deep. That's what the serious ones do.'

He grimaced apologetically at making Rory's task harder.

'That's where the body was found. Six metres down, probably more,' Rory told him.

'How did they find a body that far down? Hadn't the shaft been filled in?'

'Oh yeah. The shaft with the body in it had been filled in, but the bloke who found it had dug another shaft and found the body when he tunnelled sideways.'

'Phew, that's pretty incredible. I mean incredible all round. Incredible that a body was dropped in a deep hole in the first place and then for someone to accidentally find it by randomly digging another deep hole and tunnelling to that exact spot … I reckon that's beyond anyone's imagination. I bet that's given you blokes plenty to think about. I mean …' He looked into space and thought about what he imagined puzzled the police.

'What?' Rory asked.

'Well, are you looking for a gemstone fossicker who just happens to have a body to get rid of and takes the opportunity to kill two birds with one stone … sorry … the pun's not intended.'

'Not a bad pun, though,' Rory smiled.

'Hmm, but I don't buy my own theory. It could be a fossicker, of course, but more likely, it's someone entirely unconnected. Someone in the know or someone who got lucky and arrived after the fossicker left but before the hole was filled in.'

'How is there a gap? I thought the hole had to be filled in before you leave.'

'Theoretically. The place is hardly ever monitored, though, and it's a mighty task to fill a hole when you go really deep. There're a few old-timers who get Hal Rogers to bring his front-end-loader tractor in and do it for them. Hal's a local landholder over on the east side. You're not allowed to use machinery when you're searching for gems, but filling in a hole is not searching for gems, so I suppose it's legit. What it does mean though is, if Hal can't be there straight away, there can be days or weeks when the hole remains unfilled with no one around. That's your opportunity to drop a body in, shovel in enough soil to cover it — unbeknownst to Hal, of course — then Hal happens along and completes the job for you. Bob's your uncle.'

Rory nodded sagely as he took in Mack's cogitating.

'Do you know any of the fossickers?'

'I've met a few over the years, but I wouldn't say I know any of them. Some years we pop in at Easter when there's always a few around. Have a yarn and see what they're still finding. A couple of the regulars liked to leave some of their heavier gear here when they head home … so I can keep an eye on it for them. Over near the wool shed, there's an earth moving scraper used for filling in holes. That's been there for at least five years. It belongs to Cyril someone from somewhere in the Wimmera. He looked too old for the game even then, so I don't reckon I'll see him again. I don't know his surname, and we didn't do phone numbers. Not with something like that. You know.'

'Yeah. It's a country thing. Right?'

'Exactly.'

Rory brought up Michelle's number on his phone and hit dial. It was time for the post-coital phone conversation.

'*Hi.*'

'Hi,' he answered. They were both smiling. They both knew it and were taking their time.

'*Where are you?*'

'I just dropped Tahlia off in Dunkeld. She's getting a ride back to Halls Gap with a Parks Victoria crew. I've got a three-hour drive ahead of me.'

'*It sounds like you wanted to revisit the scene of our own crime. The criminal psychologist in me tells me you want to relive the act.*'

'I don't think you need a degree to tell you that. How about you? Do you fancy a return visit?'

'*You'll have to ask me again to see, won't you?*'

He could picture her smiling.

'Hmm.'

'*Well, that's the smuggest "Hmm" I ever heard.*'

'Hmm. Where are you?'

'*At the supermarket. My daughter and her partner are coming for dinner tonight. I have to cook.*'

'I was going to pop in on my way through. I'll catch you over the weekend then.'

'*Oh, I'm sorry, Rory, I promised Audrey I'd go to the Daylesford market with her. I thought it would just be on Saturday, but I think she's booked an Airbnb.*'

She "thinks" Audrey booked an Airbnb. Her being vague gave Rory pause.

'All right then ....'

'I'll be back Sunday, but then I have to bone up for the seminar in Sydney. I'm flying up there early in the week. My life isn't normally this committed, but ... How about I give you a call.'

Early in the week? Not specifically on Monday or Tuesday? Without warning, their Dunkeld-reminiscing had sunk without trace. Rory felt the caution Radiohead's Ill Wind playing out. "Keep your distance", they had sung.

'I'll be *Thinking About You'*, he answered with another Radiohead song title popping into his head.

Chapter 8

'Fucking podcasts. Now every man … and woman, and their fucking dog want to tell us how to do our job,' Inspector Bourke announced as he barged into his own office. The big olive-skinned man with a bald dome thundered past Rory and Cockburn, slammed a manilla folder on his desk and came to a bristling halt, staring out the window.

Rory and Cockburn had been on time to brief Bourke about the gem-site murder, only to find Bourke had been summoned to the commissioner's office. "Gem of a Murder" was how it appeared in the Sun-Herald headline that Monday morning. The page three story was accompanied by a picture of Terry, gleefully displaying his prized black crystal in its thunderegg.

Bourke's unanticipated absence gave Rory and Cockburn plenty of time to wander downstairs to the coffee cart and equip themselves with — in Rory's case — a disposable cup of double-shot long black. Cockburn chose a cappuccino.

Bourke swung around.

'Did you get me one of those?'

Rory and Cockburn's nonplussed looks gave him their answers before either could form words.

'Fran, I need a coffee.'

The rear of Bourke's PA was visible through the office's glass front. Without turning around, she raised her right hand, then gathered her bag to leave.

'Candice and Kelly, whoever the fuck they are, have dug up the Ursula McShaw murder and done a podcast that's about to make it into the top-ten. In my day, the only top-ten thing people cared about — or paid money for — was vinyl records. Whatever happened to music, for God's sake … and records? And what makes "Candice and Kelly" authorities on anything? All they're doing is Googling away in their kitchen, looking for anything they can that makes us look like shit. Why don't they do a podcast on getting evidence that will stand up against smartarse lawyers fabricating arguments about self-preservation or mental impairment? … or fucking duress? … how the system lets someone who pulls the actual trigger get off … or lets them get it downgraded to manslaughter. Fucking podcasts. You're gonna have to deal with this one, Rory. The minister's advisor's in the commissioner's ear big time. Listen to the fucking thing and prepare a briefing.'

He sunk into the chair behind his desk and let his ire subside to a frown. Rory and Cockburn took it as a signal to sit in the two chairs facing Bourke across his desk. Rory responded.

'I spoke to Candice and Kelly when they were making the podcast. I played a straight bat. I know everyone knows Dwyer did it — which doesn't make us smell like roses — but the public prosecutor's office won't touch it without a smoking gun handed to them on a platter. That's whose ear the minister's advisor should be in. Get the prosecutors to run the case and fail. Let them be the bad cop for a change.' He paused to let his own rant sink in, then added, 'Anyway, I reckon I've just cut another potential podcast off at the pass …'

'Whoaaaa. One disaster at a time. I've had enough ambushes for one morning. What's going on with this gemstone thing?'

Cockburn jumped in, keen to own it.

'Exactly as you read in the paper. No ID and no missing locals that fit the bill. We're waiting for pathology and for a technical match. DNA or dental. They haven't put a timeline on it yet, but unofficially, she's been down there less than ten years … probably closer to four or five. They don't think the blow on the head killed her. They're exploring asphyxia. Not something that blocked off the airway, more a case of running out of oxygen.'

'You mean she was buried alive?' Rory asked.

'Funny enough, they can rule that out too. She was probably held in a confined space. Environmental suffocation is the term they're using.'

Bourke showed no sign of being appeased.

'And I hear forensic protocols went out the window when the body was shifted. Is that gonna fuck this up in court?'

'Dunno about that. The body was already at ground level when I arrived.'

Cockburn was hastening to place himself out of that picture. Rory came clean.

'I suppose Damon Rich is an old mate of yours?' Rory speculated, remembering how Bourke had been informed about the body being found.

'It doesn't matter how I found out. Is it gonna be a problem?'

'If the body wasn't removed when and how it was, it'd still be at the bottom of that shaft waiting for some commercial mining outfit to travel there and make the place safe enough for you to authorise someone to go down there. And the division's budget would be at least twenty thousand bucks the poorer. And no, I can't see anything court-challengeable arising out of it.'

Bourke leant back in his chair. His frown lessened slightly. Cockburn turned to look cynically at Rory.

'Good. A bit of calculated common sense. I haven't seen enough of that lately. What are the theories on how it got there?'

Cockburn jumped in for another go.

'The official rules at the site are: when you're finished fossicking, you have to re-fill the hole you dug. So, we have to find whoever dug that hole where the body was buried, which is not the hole via which the body was found. The bloke who found the body tunnelled sideways from another hole into the bottom of the hole where the body was found, which would'a been filled in years ago. That's how the body was found.'

Bourke looked to Rory for interpretation.

'That's pretty much right, except, when Gary says hole, he's referring to shafts six or seven metres deep … and they don't always get refilled straightaway like they're supposed to. Sometimes they're left unattended or pretty much abandoned until one of the locals brings his front-end loader tractor over to do the job. That gives anyone else an opportunity to drop a body down there and cover it with a few shovelfuls of clay. That sounds a more likely scenario than a killer spending weeks sinking a shaft, hunting for gems as he goes, with the overriding purpose of disposing of a body that's all the while sitting in the back of his ute.'

'Where'd you come up with all that?' Cockburn snapped.

'When I was leaving, I called into the nearest farm. The bloke there told me. He also told me it'd be no easy task to find out who dug the hole — not that the person who dug the hole is likely to be the killer — but they could tell us when the hole was dug and if or when it might have been left unattended before it was refilled. The gem site is remote and un-signposted. There's no record of who comes or when they come. Apart from the odd public holiday, there's rarely more than one or two there at the same time. There's no network that encompasses more than a few fossickers, not even online. We can start chasing it down, but we might be better off waiting for the body to be ID'd. That'll give us something concrete to work on.'

'So, it's a new case, blank canvas,' Bourke mused as Fran came in and handed him the takeaway coffee.

'No trouble,' she said with breezy sarcasm as she left.

'Jesus, Fran. Sorry.' He sipped the coffee.

'Okay. You run with this Gary. Wait for an ID and take it from there. You happy to get back to the cold case workload Rory, and review this fucking Ursula McShaw case yet again? You'd better make sure these sheilas haven't dug up something we don't know about.'

'Sure. But at some stage, I want to get back to the Grampians on a missing person case. That's the possible staved-off podcast I started to tell you about … although that's not what it's about.'

'Then what is it about?' Bourke asked.

'The local cultural heritage specialist that you hooked me up with. Her older brother went missing down there a few years ago. At the time, her family, who live in Queensland, got the bum's rush. That's according to her … I haven't pulled the file yet. Anyway, she's older now and not long outta university. She happened to get a job in the area, and she's started sniffing around. She's still getting the brush-off from our local colleagues, but she has unearthed some evidence that I don't think can be ignored. We might have a case of "presumed to have met with foul-play" on our hands.'

Cockburn reverted to type.

'That Aboriginal chick's got a brother who's gone missing? Probably gone walkabout if you ask me.'

Rory turned to Cockburn and held out both hands as a magician would for a ta-dah moment or as quiz show hostesses do when displaying a prize to the viewing audience.

'Thanks for making my point Gary,' Rory said, then turned to Bourke to continue. 'That's it. That's exactly the response she and her family received. Candice and Kelly can come to you for that quote when they do the podcast. I'm sure the minister's advisor won't have much to say about that.'

'Okay, Rory, you made your point … and Gary …' Bourke shook his head with hopelessness.

Cockburn stood to leave and give a parting shot. 'Jesus, you two. I'm outta here. I've got a real case to deal with.'

Bourke waited for him to be out of earshot.

'Don't tell me. This cultural heritage woman, she fancied you as a knight in shining armour to resurrect the case and treat it seriously?'

'What can I say? She's only ever encountered the Cockburn variety of cops.'

'Yeah, well, don't let her anywhere near Cockburn. I don't need HR on my back for something like that.'

'Too late. They've already met and gone toe-to-toe. But don't worry. She gave as good as she got … and she's not precious about what comes out of Gary's mouth. If she was, he'd already be in deep shit.'

'Yeah,' Bourke frowned at the thought. 'Okay then. Check out the missing persons file and verify the new evidence you reckon she's found. Let me know if we have enough to take it on as a possible homicide, and I'll square it off with Missing Persons. And let me know, even if we haven't got a possible homicide … so I can give whoever dealt with it in the first place a kick up the arse. Don't want to leave podcast fodder lying around, even if it's not on my patch.'

'Okay.'

'And one more thing. I know you. So, if you're down that way and you find out stuff about the gem-site case, you pass it on to Gary. It's his case. I don't need you two at loggerheads again.'

Chapter 9

Tahlia walked into the front yard of her share-house to make the call. The share-house was a rare commodity in Halls Gap. More commonly, owners listed their houses on Airbnb for holiday letting. Fortunately for Tahlia, the parents of one of her co-tenants owned the house. The downside was, they all had to vacate the place once or twice a year when his parents chose to use the holiday house themselves. Painfully, that usually occurred during peak periods when the youth hostel and camping grounds were packed.

Sandy soil and bracken gave the weatherboard cottage a beach house feel, and that was no accident. The Grampians began their existence as a shallow seabed — attested to by fossils of shells and fish spines. Before man's ancestral life-forms morphed into mammals, that sea floor tilted like giant trap doors being accessed from beneath. The resulting peaks and escarpments of sandstone then set about the never-to-be-completed task of eroding. Grain by grain, wind and rain plucked a carpet of sand upon which the captivating lower reaches flourished, including Halls Gap.

Craggy cliff faces below the famed Pinnacle lookout eclipsed any outlook from the backdoor of the cottage. The front yard, on the other hand, fell away towards the valley floor, affording a serene panorama of the Mount William Range across the glen. Tahlia eschewed the bench seat placed precisely for that viewing pleasure and stood, dialling her mother's number. It would not be a relaxed call.

'*Hello.*'

'Hi Mum, it's me,' she answered and began pacing.

'*Oh. Hello Tah, I was just about to have a nap. How are you?*'

'I'm good. I'm back home now. I've finished that job with the cops. Like I told you, the body wasn't a bloke, and it turns out it had nothing to do with any of the stuff I usually deal with … job-wise, I mean … but it was a good experience. You know. Now it's back to my normal job tomorrow.'

She chose to say, "it wasn't a bloke", unable to voice the words, "it wasn't Ricky".

'*But it coulda had somethin' to do with you, couldn't it? And even though it wasn't Ricky, I still sensed a bad spirit about the whole thing. I'm glad it's behind you, Tah.*'

'I know, Mum, but I shouldn't've told you in the first place. I just had a rush of blood or something. Now that I think about it, a body chucked in a mine shaft was always gonna be some white person shit. And it's not like something like that's gonna fall in my lap again, so there's no lesson to learn. I'm just gonna go back to work tomorrow and get on with life. Okay?'

'*Oh yeah? And what about this cop you took a shine to. Did you bring Ricky up with him, or is that all over too? Cause if it is ….*'

'What do you mean, "if it is"?'

'*Donna, who I see a bit of at the cultural centre, her girl Lorinda went missing too, up near here, not long before Ricky. Anyway, a journalist from Brisbane popped down to see her about it. She does stuff on the radio. She's doing a story about Donna's daughter. She reckons there's plenty of others like her and the cops treat 'em as if they're all invisible.*

'*Donna told her about Ricky, and she told Donna I should speak to her. Victoria's too far away for her to do anything about it herself, but she knows someone in Victoria she can tell about it. You know, another journalist down there.*'

The line went quiet, and Tahlia stopped pacing.

'*Are you there, Tahlia?*'

'Don't.'

'*Whatya mean "don't"?*'

'I mean, don't raise it with that journalist. Detective James said he's going to have a look at the case. That's what I phoned you about. I need to get a couple of details from you and email them to him. I don't want you to muck this up on me, Mum. Okay?'

'*I dunno, Tah. No one has shown a breath of interest until now, and how many years has it been? How long can hope last? Do you think the cops are gonna suddenly change their spots after this long? They haven't picked up the phone in all that time, have they? This is a chance to shake things up, and I reckon we shouldn't waste it. I really don't.'*

'Mum, a journalist — if that's what she is — is not going to find Ricky. The best outcome she can offer you is to rattle the cage enough to embarrass the cops into pulling their finger out. And you know what? I've already done that. Not embarrassed them, but Detective James is gonna look into it … and not in a reluctant way, which could happen if you shame them into taking action. How would you feel about that? Having them simply going through the motions again.'

'Detective James, so you're on first-name terms then?'

'No. That's his surname. Look, Mum. I don't know if he'll do any good or not. All I know is he's not a dickhead cop, which is as good as a blackfella can hope for. He might even be a bit better than "not a dickhead". Who knows? He listened, and then he agreed to take a look … on the spot. So, the last thing I think we should do is anything that pisses him off.'

'So, you're asking me to trust your instinct?'

'I am, Mum. But don't put it all on me like that. I said I've got no idea how he'll go, but …'

'But what? What does your heart tell you about him?'

Tahlia stared hard at the distant Mount William Range to gather her thoughts.

'I get the feeling he's been damaged, but he's done a pretty good job of putting himself back together, like. There's a kind of sadness that lingers, not in a pitiable way, though. Like he knows hurt far too well to hurt anyone himself … maybe it's empathy, I don't know … I think I'm rambling.'

'Nah, Tah. It's me you're talking to. I know what you're saying, even if you don't, okay? I'll keep Ricky's story to myself, but ...' She paused to emphasise her next point, 'I'm not gonna throw that woman's phone number away either.'

Chapter 10

Rory stretched out behind his desk. His right calf rested on one end of the worktop, an elbow on the other, chin in hand. The YouTube version of Candice and Kelly's Ursula McShaw murder podcast played on the desktop computer. It was background. His gaze had shifted from the screen display — the podcast's title page overlaid with a flickering band of an audio waveform. Rory's attention had also drifted from the audio stream. The content may have been high octane fuel for a layperson's unalloyed rage, but he knew the story too well.

Furthermore, however compelling it was being portrayed, he knew that a much-needed silver bullet of demonstrable, irrefutable evidence was never going to crack a mention. There was one positive he could mention in his written briefing for the commissioner: the heightened public interest could bring forth a hitherto unknown witness. Now he needed an eloquent way to say: "… but don't hold your breath".

I bet they're doing it.

His wandering gaze had settled on a flirting couple in the open-office floor plan beyond the glass front of his small office. They were the sole occupants of a three-desk pod, sectioned off with low partitions. The bloke sat at his desk. She sat on the end of it — on his side. Amid their over-smiley chatter, he stroked her leg. She kept turning to the rest of the busy, occupied office, smiling with ebullient joy, knowing others on the floor couldn't see what was happening below the surface. They were both oblivious to Rory's presence behind them — which in their defence, was seldom.

His office was at the rear of the IT branch on the floor immediately below the homicide branch. Except for Rory, everyone else on the floor was a civilian employee with a boffin bent. When Rory returned to the job after a year off, he jumped at the chance of a bolt-hole away from the fray of the homicide squad proper, a place where he couldn't have been more persona-non-grata. He was the perceived culprit of Heidi Lester's career ending injury; he was being rewarded with time off for the supposed "disorder" he acquired from simply doing what he was paid to do, and he scored the coveted "light duties" role of a one-man cold cases unit into the bargain. The latter was a deliberate strategy to ease him back into "real" police work.

His spell of accidental voyeurism was broken by the chime of an incoming email. The pop-up box told him it was from Tahlia Lock.

He paused the podcast and opened Tahlia's email. It was the details he'd asked her for about her missing bother. The email was laid out as a list of concise dot points. No chit-chat at the beginning or end. It was signed off: "Regards Tahlia". As businesslike as. He pressed the Print button, then logged onto the internal database to retrieve the case and bring it up on screen.

Ricky Lock. No second name. Ricky Lock. Not a name you'd expect to see as an author of an anthropological journal article, Rory pondered, then pronounced himself *guilty. Did that careless assumption trickle down into the police response?*

The obvious ID details followed — *home address, age, physical appearance, mobile phone*, as well as last known whereabouts and a coloured photo displaying Ricky's unmistakable Aboriginality. Below that stretched a list of blank fields that included: *what the missing person was last seen wearing, intended travel arrangements, habits and places he/she frequented, social media accounts, banking information, behavioural change/emotional problems, medication, reported missing before, friends and acquaintances.* The final *Additional notes* field stated: "Departed the youth hostel without paying for his accommodation". A separate Authority for Media Release document signed by Ricky's mum was also on the electronic database. Its *distribution details* were blank. What was also missing was any mention of Ricky's vehicle — both at the time Ricky went missing and down the track when, as Tahlia had told him, the vehicle showed up in an accident.

A cynic might conclude that the database version of Ricky's disappearance well and truly confirmed Tahlia's story about police prejudice and dismissiveness. Rory felt obliged to give it the benefit of the doubt. The bareness of the electronic file could just as likely be the result of no one finding time to sit and enter other data that may or may not have been collected and amassed on a hard copy. Maybe the cops dealing with the case had been waiting for something to come along and take them back to work on the file … and that something never came. Equally plausible: they simply added the minimum details required to have the case listed on the Federal Police's national database of missing persons.

Rory typed a request for retrieval of a hard-copy file into his computer and un-paused the Candice and Kelly podcast. Ricky would have to wait a day or two.

The next welcome interruption — any interruption was welcome — came with an office phone call from Cockburn.

'Hello. Detective Sergeant James.'

'*So, you are down in your burrow today?*'

'I'm well, thank you, and yourself?'

'*We've got an ID on the gem-site body. Bourke wants you in on it too. You wanna come up here now?*'

Rory made his way past the flirting couple.

'Morning,' Rory said, smiling.

Their open mouths were still waiting for words as he entered the stairwell.

Bourke had extracted himself from behind his computer to the coffee table and tub chairs squeezed into the corner of his office. Cockburn was leaning forward to hold a single sheet of paper face down on the table. Also on the table were their two empty cups and a space-age looking conference-call phone — pretty much a loud speaker with a dial-pad and no handset.

'That was quick,' Rory said as he came in — referring to the dead body's ID having been established.

'Rory,' Bourke acknowledged as Rory made a bee line for the remaining empty chair. He waited for Rory to be seated, then gave Cockburn the nod. Cockburn flipped the page and left it on the table.

'DNA match and dental match. Beyond all doubt,' Cockburn said. 'They also confirmed she died of environmental suffocation and ruled out being buried alive. Most likely, she spent her final hours in a confined space. My guess is a car boot, by the way.'

The woman's photograph occupied almost half the single-page printout. Blonde-ish, tasselled hair fell to her shoulders. To Rory, she looked to be exactly of that unfathomable age between forty and fifty, perhaps on the younger end of that spectrum. Her dark eyes were tending to be narrow. First impression? *Well-groomed and perhaps better-looking than the flash-photography was giving her credit for*, he concluded in his head. In large, bold print above the photograph was her name, Gloria Vella. Below the headshot were about a dozen headings with one-or-two-word responses — "Missing Since", "Gender, Height", and the like. The response for the bottom category, "Circumstances", ran for a paragraph. Rory picked it up for a closer look. He began reading and mumbling a conversation with himself.

'Gloria Vella, not hit with the ugly stick … missing for more than four years, forensics guessed that bit right. From East Hills in New South Wales. Wow, a suburb of Sydney, who'd have guessed? I suppose she had to be from somewhere, though … last seen driving home from the supermarket. Found to be missing several days later when she couldn't be raised on the phone. Her car was parked in the driveway. Grave concerns are held for her welfare and safety.'

Rory lifted his eyes from the page.

'What's the story?'

Cockburn answered.

'Nothing so far. That's all we've got. A printout from the feds' National Missing Persons Coordination Centre.'

Bourke picked up the story.

'Gary tracked down the New South Wales cop who worked on the case. We've got a conference call organised. You ready to go?'

'Yeah.'

'Bourke punched the number in. Pressed the button with a green handset symbol.

'*Detective Sergeant Oglethorpe,*' a female voice announced. Bourke and Rory looked at each other, acknowledging the same thought — a woman.

'Hello, Detective Sergeant. Inspector Richard Bourke here, Homicide Squad Melbourne. I'm on speakerphone with Detective Sergeants Gary Cockburn and Rory James.'

'*Morning all. It's Rochelle, by the way.*'

'Morning,' Rory and Cockburn said in unison. Bourke pushed on.

'Thanks, Rochelle. I presume you've been told we found the body of Gloria Vella. It's a definite DNA and dental records match. The Fed's national website tells us bugger all else. We're hoping you can put us in the picture about what we're dealing with here.'

'Sure. From memory, Gloria Vella went missing over four years ago. She was married, but her husband was working away at the time — lots of times, actually. He was — probably still is — a mining geologist. He works all over Australia. One weekend while he was working away, he couldn't raise her on the phone. On the Monday, she didn't show up at work. Eventually, he got one of their friends to go around to the house. That's when they came to us.'

She drew breath. Rory had begun making notes. Bourke prompted her to go on.

'Then what?'

'Nothing as far as a result or any evidence goes. The house was in its normal state. No sign of struggle or evidence of anyone else having been in the house. Vanished without a trace, as they say.'

'And what about her personal life?' Bourke asked.

'No kids, and it emerged during the investigation that her husband was misbehaving while he was working away.'

'By misbehaving, you don't mean he was caught parking in a disabled bay?' Cockburn said.

'No, I don't. He was regularly having sexual intercourse with another woman,' she was required to spell out.

'Did his wife know?' Bourke asked.

'*We think so.*'

'And that's it?' Cockburn pressed.

'*No. Of course not. The case copped plenty of public interest. We produced heaps of media stuff, and the media ran hard with it. They still resurrect the story from time to time and run it in the weekend magazines. The implication is always, "did he do it?"*'

'And did he?' Bourke again.

'*Until this point in time, I was tending towards saying no, if anything. What I can tell you for certain, though, is, at the time of her disappearance, he was working somewhere near the Grampians. That's where I understand her body was found. He was working in the field, involved in surveying and testing for a mineral exploration licence. Because there is no precise day of her disappearance, there were gaps in his alibi where technically, he may have had time to drive to Sydney and back ... but there was no evidence. No sightings on all the service stations and other CCTV we gathered. No toll road records, speed camera stuff. Nothing like that. Zilch. And he was convincing. The only doubt I ever had about him was: he wouldn't front the cameras and do an appeal to the public.*

'*I guess what I'm saying is: her body turns up down there where he was working at the time ... well, it'd be pretty hard to draw any other conclusion.*'

Rory stopped making notes to offer a suggestion.

'Maybe she travelled to the Grampians, not the other way around,'

'*We thought of that, even though we never had a body. The only problem with that theory was, her car was still in Sydney, and there were no records of her using public transport. Anyway, you're the ones who have got the body now, and I can tell you, you've got yourself a real problem to solve.*'

Bourke took over.

'The husband. We're going to have to speak to him ourselves. Does he still live there?'

'*Yeah, Travis Vella. Same house ... and his love interest from back then now lives there with him. I don't think they're married, though. Probably because technically, he's still married to Gloria.*'

'I've already organised the paperwork for someone up there to let him know about his wife.'

'*That'll probably end up being my job. I can let you know how he reacts if you like.*'

'Appreciate that, Rochelle. I'll also do the paperwork for Rory or Gary to come up there, Interview her husband ....'

'*Travis Vella?*' Rochelle interjected.

'... yeah. Interview Travis Vella. Share information, maybe visit the house ... all that.'

'*I'll look forward to it,*'

'Okay. Maybe we'll leave it at that for now. Anything else you can think of, Rochelle? Rory? Gary?'

Shakes of the head all around.

'Alright. Thanks for your help. We'll catch up again soon.'

'*No problem. Bye, gents.*'

Bourke disconnected, and the dial tone sounded. Cockburn felt safe to talk.

'She sounds friendly. I wonder what she looks like. Do you know how old she is?'

'You fucking behave yourself if you want to fly to Sydney,' Bourke said.

'Just sayin'.'

'Well, just don't. You fancy a trip to Sydney too, Rory?'

'I'll be heading back to the Grampians on this missing person thing. Gary can have Rochelle to himself. I will keep chasing the Gloria Vella thing up while I'm down that way, though … now we know who we're dealing with.'

Bourke stood.

'Good. That sounds like a plan. Keep me posted on anything major.'

Chapter 11

Rory checked the time. He knew that wherever Michelle was, she'd be out of bed by now. He dialled. The dial tone sounded. He got the machine … again. He knew he was being paranoid for a reason. Something had turned on a pin's head at the end of their last phone conversation. As one PTSD sufferer to another, he knew he wasn't imagining it — whatever it was.

He pocketed his mobile phone and wandered up the office stairs to collect his internal mail. He steered clear of Cockburn, said a "g'day" to Fran outside Bourke's office. Her eyes lifted from the screen to shoot a beaming smile. Her fingers kept typing. Her eyes soon caught up again. He grabbed the slim Ricky Lock file from his inwards mail slot and engaged in two more perfunctory "hi's" before reaching the stairwell. Workplace relations done for the day.

He dropped the file onto his desk, dropped into his seat, gazed at the IT world beyond his doorstep, and met the eyes of flirter-woman. This time she was aware of Rory's presence and remained safely on the other side of her co-flirter's desk. She was leaning over the partition screen. Rory swore to himself that she mouthed, "He's there", to the leg-fondler.

The slimness of Ricky Lock's missing-person file gave the story away before Rory opened the cover. The initial report form included the basics, as well as that alluding *Additional note*: "Departed the youth hostel without paying for his accommodation".

Nevertheless, the narrative on the hard copy file had some info that hadn't made it onto the electronic version. It indicated that Ricky was absent for a couple of days before his travelling companions realised he wasn't coming back. Apparently, Ricky had begun going his own way. Ricky's alternative interests had been paraphrased on the file: "while his travelling companions remained drawn to the Grampians ancient rock art sites, Ricky began exploring the area's Aboriginal history since European occupation".

He had obviously departed the hostel by vehicle. His silver Hyundai. His friends didn't know the registration number, but someone had looked it up and entered the number on the file. Ricky's backpack was still at the hostel, minus whatever he travelled with on the day he left — laptop, phone, wallet etc.

Rory was surprised to see a media release had been prepared, then un-surprised when he noticed the date — six weeks after he had gone missing. It appeared to have been instigated by Ricky's mum showing up in Victoria to complain about inaction. There was no record of whether the story appeared in any media outlet.

The most recent record on file was a note about Ricky's car being involved in the crash at Warrnambool, six months after Ricky disappeared. It mentioned that one of the occupants was also Aboriginal. The survivor of the crashed vehicle's two occupants insisted they found the car abandoned. That kinda corroborated Tahlia's story. He logged onto his email to re-read the dot-point details Tahlia had sent him about Ricky's disappearance. He realised that her email did not include contact details for the car crash survivor. He went back to the hard copy file. It concluded: "It could not be discounted that the vehicle had remained in Aboriginal circles since Ricky Lock was reported missing. No further action taken". No one had actually written "gone walkabout" on the file, but it was writ large between every line.

Rory made a to-do list.

1. Have the comms branch do a search to see if the media release received an airing by any outlets.

2. Retrieve the road accident file for the crash Ricky's car was involved in at Warrnambool. Obtain contact details for the car crash survivor.

3. Contact Ricky's colleagues who travelled with him to the Grampians. He wrote down their names — Lucas Curry and Leona Craig — and their mobile numbers.

Having actioned the first two items via email, he dialled the number for Lucas Curry. It made an unfamiliar tone that suggested the number no longer existed. He dialled Leona Craig instead.

'*Hello. Leona speaking.*'

'Hello, Leona. This is Detective Sergeant Rory James with the Victoria Police. I'm calling you about Ricky Lock.'

'*Oh ... has something happened? ... Have they found him?*'

Her manner became more hesitant with each word. Like she was really asking, "Have they found his body?"

'No, I'm afraid Ricky hasn't been located, but the case is being reviewed. Because I wasn't involved in the initial investigation, I'd like to catch up for a chat if you have the time. To hear the story first hand. Do you mind me asking where you're based these days?'

'*I'm happy ... Well, not happy, but I'm okay with having a talk. And I live in Melbourne. I work at the Melbourne Museum. That's where I am right now. Do I have to come to the police station?*'

'No. It won't be an interview as such. It really is just a chat. Can we meet somewhere for coffee? Your usual if you like, or somewhere away from familiar eyes if you'd rather. Your call.'

'*Oh, I don't have any reason to skulk around,*' she said defensively. '*Why don't we meet at the museum café. If you give me a bit of notice, I can take a break and meet you there any time. Well, any time between eight-thirty and five o'clock.*'

'Wonderful. I can jump on a tram right now. Give me about forty minutes. Is that okay?'

He kept catching her off guard. Another response came that began with "Oh".

'*Oh, of course. I'll see you at about half-past.*'

'Half-past then. I'm not the uniform variety cop, so I'll be the regular bloke who looks like a cop.'

She gave her phone a non-plussed look after Rory ended the call.

The tram ride across the city would have been a leisurely diversion if not for the crammed contingent of passengers. Firstly, those arriving downtown. Then the throng setting forth to the northern suburbs on route eighty-six — a drop-punt shy of being the longest on the network.

Rory alighted on first sighting of the invitingly shady Carlton Gardens. There was time enough to enjoy a stroll past the Royal Exhibition Building. The grand historic showpiece of Australia's pre-Canberra parliament venue now shared the entry plaza to the neo-constructivist cool of the Melbourne Museum. Opened in 2000, the museum always reeked of appeasement for 1990s premier Jeff Kennett's breathtaking cost-cutting — 350 schools and 7,000 teachers to begin with. With that tidy earner and privatisation of anything that moved — power, gas, prisons, ambulance, even the TAB — he could afford a new museum, and some. The trade-off also gave Melbourne other architectural bravura, like Federation Square and the big cantilevered cheese-stick on the airport freeway.

It was Rory's first close-up visit to the museum, and he had to admit the architect's bold creation had settled in nicely. Perhaps it always had. *How have I not been here before?* The strong architecture continued inside to the café, sited with a view through the mammoth glass facade. Leona sat waiting with her hands clasped on one of the front tables. Their enquiring faces — and in Leona's case, her security lanyard — told them they were who they were each expecting. Leona had a studious face, or was he imagining that? Rory wondered. She wore a dark dress over a black short-sleeved top and black tights. Her complexion — genuine Gen Y clear. Hair — dyed bright red and woven into a thick casual plait.

They both smiled, introduced themselves and ordered coffees. Rory paid, and they adjourned to a window table. The place was far from busy, but the cavernous scale of the seated areas nonetheless added privacy to their conversation.

'I also tried to contact Lucas Curry, but his phone number seemed defunct,' Rory began.

'That'd be right. Lucas went overseas. Chasing the archaeologist's long-lost civilisation dream from what I can tell. The last Facebook posting I saw, he was in Mexico.'

'And is this your dream?' Rory cast his eyes to their surrounds.

'Maybe part of it. I've got a temporary position in the invertebrate palaeontology department. I love it. Like, I'm learning heaps, but it'd crush me if I thought my working life would start and end in the same place.'

'That's a millennial thing, isn't it?'

'Maybe. It's just how it's worked out so far for me.'

Both reached for their coffee to take a first sip. Rory removed a notepad from his jacket pocket and placed it on the table. He left it closed.

'Can we get down to it then? Tell me about that Grampians trip and how it came about that Ricky went missing.'

'Okay then. Umm. Let me think. Umm … I remember Ricky and I arrived on a Friday night. I'd have to check the date. We drove up from Melbourne in his car. Lucas had something on Friday night, and he came up on Saturday. Lucas had to go to his dad's birthday or something like that. That was important because, like, if we all went in Ricky's car, Lucas and I would have been stranded when Ricky never showed up.'

'I don't need dates. We have all that. Just tell me what happened while you were there,' Rory said.

'We were mainly checking out rock shelters that had once been occupied or had rock art in them. It wasn't a dig or anything like that. We weren't able to do anything that disturbed the sites. One of our tutors had set us up with a local guide, and he was happy to talk us through the history and significance of the various shelters. His name was Leonard Dalton, Lenny. Lenny knew remote sites, away from those on the guided tours and maps. That was the best bit for me. The privilege of being taken to those sites, untouched since the Europeans arrived on the scene.'

She paused for another sip.

Rory smiled, leaving an opening for her to continue.

'Lenny also knew a lot of the more recent history of the area, and Ricky took a real interest in that. When I say recent, I mean since European settlement. Lenny knew stories that had been passed down about how Aborigines and settlers interacted, not usually in a good way, and Ricky would press him for details. It obviously appealed to him on an Indigenous level, as well as academically.'

'Can you give me an idea of the kinds of things that caught his interest?'

'He was particularly intrigued by a couple of early European-settlement massacres that occurred in the Victoria Range side of the Grampians. In one incident, a newspaper of the day reported eight aborigines were killed and others wounded. The precise locations of where those atrocities took place were not mentioned, and as far as Lenny knew, they remained a mystery. Lenny had looked into it, however, and found a few clues for one episode, like how far the site was from Mount Zero — over twenty kilometres, from memory. He also had a description of the place. I think it was referred to as a bight in the mountains where a rapid creek emerged, running over rocks. Armed with that info, we thought the place would jump out at us. So, Lenny took us all to what he thought was the general area.

'When we got there, we realised that identifying the location was a hopeless quest. We didn't know if the measurement from Mount Zero was by road or by a straight line on a map. Like, as the crow flies. The thing that really hindered our search, though, was the thick impenetrable scrub in those gullies. Like, we knew that when the massacre occurred, Aboriginal burn-offs would have exposed the foothill gorges as pretty dells. Nowadays, we couldn't see a metre in front of our faces. It wasn't too long before we gave the whole idea away.'

She paused her story to ask, 'Do you want to know about all this? Stop me if you don't think it's relevant.'

'I won't know if it's relevant or not until I hear it, but it is interesting. Tell me how you think it's relevant to Ricky.'

'Well, that was something that Ricky didn't want to let go of. He went back there on his own … more than once, I think. And, not long before he disappeared, he said he'd met up with a local farmer, an old-timer who told him he knew about another site. Another killing site that was not on any record. The incident in the Victoria Range was reported because it was led by police chasing a group of Aborigines who had stolen sheep. But settlers often took such matters into their own hands, and when those killings happened, a code of silence was not uncommon. One squatter sacked his shepherds for leaking it.

'The farmer that Ricky spoke to reckons that among his ancestors' private letters was a fairly detailed account of a multiple killing committed by one of his ancestor's neighbours on their sheep run. He told Ricky he was familiar with the area and he could decipher the location from the description in the letter. I don't know if Ricky eventually went there or not, though. I think he was waiting to see the letter or something.'

'What about the farmer's ancestors? If they knew about it, would they have been part of the code of silence too?' Roy asked.

'Totally. To tell the truth, it preyed on my mind, and I've looked into it a bit since Ricky went missing. What I found was: when Europeans were investigated or brought to trial, other Europeans were reluctant to testify, even those grieved by the outrages. Of course, any evidence from Aborigines was inadmissible. None of that, however, stemmed settlers' glee when police had a hand in the matter, like the Victoria Range massacre. Newspapers editorialised that neighbourhood settlers were in "perfect ecstasies". That the police deserved great praise. Can you believe it?'

Rory took it as a rhetorical question. He watched a bunch of primary school children arriving outside, all wearing mini hi-vis jackets and hats. They were young enough for each to be holding a fellow student's hand and not be concerned if it were of the opposite gender. Two grownups had the role of sheepdog, one at the front, another at the rear.

'Do you know anything about the farmer Ricky spoke to or how their paths crossed? How the subject came up? There's nothing ordinary about an encounter like that, not by anyone's standards, is there?'

'No. I don't think Ricky wanted to reveal too much until he could verify the provenance. We were curious too, but we understood there was nothing to get excited about until he saw what info the guy had. Have you seen those old letters? Someone could easily misinterpret what has been written. Then the account would have to be aligned to the modern-day landscape. We, as archaeologists, knew that was never a lay-down misére. So we didn't push it. I mean, like it was only talk at that stage. Sure, it was a serious matter if it turned out to be true, but it's not something you simply take at face value. And Ricky hadn't gone missing or anything … not then. I mean, how were we to know?'

'No. Fair enough. That's not what I was getting at. I'm just thinking aloud. This "other" massacre site, though — if it exists — it wouldn't be on Crown Land like in the Grampians, would it? Wouldn't it be on land that someone owns?' he asked Leona.

'I suppose so.'

'And whoever owns that land, well they may not be pleased to have it exposed? Not even after all this time?'

'Possibly so. Possibly not. I suppose that would depend on the attitude of whoever owns the land these days. If the place has stayed in the hands of the family of the original settlers, then maybe not ... or even if they didn't have a family connection, you wouldn't want to be tarred with that brush. I remember seeing a TV documentary that wanted to visit a massacre location on private land. They got short shrift and made a point of saying so. So, yeah. You're probably right. It's always going to be hairy.'

Through her thinking-out-loud process, the relevance of Rory's question dawned on Leona.

'Oh. So, you do think that it could have something to do with Ricky disappearing?'

'I've no idea. I'm only just learning about all this from you. Did you tell the police at the time?'

'I think we mentioned it, but they were more concerned about Ricky shooting through without paying his hostel bill. I think they saw that as the crime they had to solve. I don't think they even believed we were qualified archaeologists either. I think they thought we'd concocted a story to cover for Ricky. I also remember they wanted to know everything about

Ricky's car. Like that'd be their best chance to nab him for doing a runner on the hostel.'

'Did they do any follow up with you or Lucas?'

'Only once. I got a phone call more than a month later. I think Ricky's mum came down from New South Wales and gave them a serve. I could tell they knew they had a missing person on their hands by that stage, but like I could also tell they were going through the motions. I mentioned Ricky was exploring stuff on his own, but even on the phone, I could tell the woman cop wasn't writing it down. I'm pleased you're reviewing the case. I'm pleased you listen. Thank you.'

Rory lifted both hands to indicate, "just doing my job". Leona grabbed her mouth. Re-living it had caught up on her.

'We were used to him doing his own thing … then he was no longer there … ever. We left it far too late. We should have gone to the police that first morning he wasn't there. But …'

'Hey, you can't blame yourself.'

'I know, but you still think, "what if", you know?'

Another bus-load of school-goers strayed onto the entry plaza. This lot were secondary students, and the sheepdogs were fighting a losing battle. Only two students held hands, and they were of the opposite gender. Rory saw the wearied male teacher mouth, "Cut it out, you two".

'Oh. This is my group. I'm scheduled to talk to them.' Leona rose from her seat, startled.

'Here's my card. If you think of anything else ….'

Leona took it and looked. Startled again.

'Homicide?'

'That doesn't mean anything. I do cold cases, and someone let this one get far too cold.'

He watched Leona leave. Looked at his phone. *Would Michelle still be on the flight to Sydney? If I call now and she doesn't answer, would that make too many unanswered calls I'd left on her mobile? What's the awkwardness threshold for unanswered calls in a new relationship? Five? Maybe. Six? Err ….* He put his phone back in his pocket and left.

Chapter 12

When Gloria Vella went missing four and a half years earlier, it was Detective Sergeant Rochelle Oglethorpe who led the case. It was the first case she led, and she lived it. She conducted every major interview, fronted every press conference, went down every rabbit hole. When the rabbit holes ran out, and the media began making up their own, it was Rochelle who put out the bushfires. The case was her baby, and it always would be. If Gloria Vella's dead body ever showed up — no one imagined she would re-emerge alive — there was no question that Rochelle would be called upon to finally piece the jigsaw together. No one imagined otherwise. But no one imagined Gloria Vella's murdered body would be found interstate. That came out of nowhere; Gloria Vella materialising as a Victorian murder for Victoria's police to solve. Rochelle felt robbed. Oddly, the death-knock — notifying the next of kin — landed in NSW's bailiwick. Gloria

Vella may have been found in Victoria, but her next of kin remained well and truly ensconced in New South Wales. That meant Rochelle would at least get to sign the case off for New South Wales before the Vics got their hands on Travis Vella. It may be the toughest thing cops say they are called upon to do, but Rochelle wasn't going to knock back the chance of seeing Travis's reaction. Not now the body had landed smack-dab in the centre of his alibi. It wouldn't be closure for Rochelle, but it would be a moment worth grasping. Rochelle still had contacts from the initial investigation. She made discrete inquiries at Travis's workplace. He was interstate, working in the Victorian Mallee, flying home the next day. *Too bad I don't know any of this*, she justified to herself. *Otherwise, I could let the Vics know, and they could handle it in their own backyard.*

The next afternoon saw Rochelle drive into the suburb of East Hills with a uniformed policewoman. The task was never tackled solo. She knew the directions but was struck by how much the landscape had changed in half a decade. Like every post-war suburb in the desirable pockets of Sydney and Melbourne, weatherboard houses with big yards had reached their use-by dates. Sufficient original specimens remained, but not many that weren't ominously looked down upon, literally, by neighbouring whole-of-block new mega-houses or duplexes. Some brick-veneer originals simply grew a second storey. Indeed, Travis Vella's house had grown the requisite second storey. What hadn't changed at Travis's address was the treed front yard that connected seamlessly to the adjoining, equivalently treed public reserve. Rochelle remained in the car when they parked and took it all in again. *All the better to be unseen when abducting someone*, she reminded herself.

Travis had spotted them arriving and was waiting at the front door. He was still dressed in his orange high-viz top and dark work pants. Early fifties, swarthy and with a few days' growth, he'd pass for an outdoor worker in any profession.

'Rochelle. It's been a while,' he greeted her.

At some stage of the missing person process, they had arrived at first names terms.

'Hello, Travis. This is Constable Kosky. Can we come in?' Rochelle's solemness resounded.

'Sounds like you'd better.'

He led them into the lounge room. Travis's partner stood up from the sofa, holding a baby. A three-year-old on the floor had frozen mid-wooden-train set play to watch their arrival.

'You remember Carol. And this is Charlotte and Austin.'

Rochelle nodded. 'Err … can we talk somewhere?'

'Sure. As you can see, we extended the place. I've got an office through here.'

Rochelle's solemness held niceties at bay. Travis led them to the office. There were only two chairs.

'It's okay. I'll stand,' Constable Kosky said.

Travis sat on the task chair. It was swivelled away from the blank computer screen to face Rochelle.

'They've found Gloria,' Rochelle announced.

Travis's expression stilled. Rochelle waited, committed to letting the message sink in.

'Not alive, I presume?'

'No.'

121

He stilled again until the next question arrived.

'Where? How did she die? Do you know?'

'She was found buried near the Grampians in Victoria. The actual cause of death was asphyxia.'

'What? Strangled? In the Grampians?'

His mouth stayed opened. Surprise seemed genuine.

'Not strangled, as I understand it. And yes, she was found near the Grampians.'

'Oh, God? Are you sure?'

'I'm afraid DNA, and dental record put it beyond doubt.'

'No. I mean, are you sure she was found near the Grampians? Sorry. Of course, you're sure.'

'Yes. Poor Gloria. I'm sorry, Travis.'

'Yes. Poor Gloria,' he echoed, acknowledging a consideration that hadn't sprung immediately to mind. Cause of death was also taking a back seat for now. 'Poor Gloria,' he repeated. 'And buried at the Grampians? That means someone has aimed this squarely at me. They know I was working over there, and they killed her and buried her there deliberately.'

'I don't know. That'll be a matter for the Victorian police to ponder. I'm simply here to notify you about Gloria.'

Travis's head dropped, and he placed his palms on his knees. Constable Kosky shifted her weight and looked at the door. The message had been delivered. *Why are we still here*?

'Do you want to check the radio please, constable? I'll join you in a moment.'

Rochelle wanted to let it play out. With her and Travis still on first name terms, something might spill. The constable departed, not needing to be asked again.

'So now there's a murder? In Victoria.'

'You don't have to say anything, Travis. I'm just here to let you know … as Gloria's next of kin … unless your marriage has been annulled … but I assumed not.'

'Yes. We are … were still married. Although, we would have gotten a divorce if she hadn't gone missing. You know all that.'

Rochelle took it as a comment. She didn't respond.

'Oh. It's that body that was found in a gemstone site, isn't it? I saw it on the news in Victoria. I've been working down there again — further north in the Mallee. That was Gloria, wasn't it?'

Rochelle nodded.

'I know that gemstone site. They chose well, I have to say.'

Rochelle cocked her head to suggest it might not be a prudent thing to say.

'I was a geologist carrying out a thorough survey of the area. That was my job. There's no way I could deny knowing about the place. I've been there. God …'

He looked at the floor and shook his head, and kept shaking his head.

'I'm going to leave now, Travis. I'll let the Victorian police know that you've been informed. I imagine Gloria's identity will soon be made public. You'll want to be prepared for the media when they get that. I can delay it a bit if you want to go somewhere else or send Carol and the kids away. The Victorian police also have your details, so ….'

'Yeah …'

He stopped looking at the floor and lifted his head to Rochelle.

'Just so you know. I didn't do it.'

'Just tell the truth,' she told him.

'There goes my trip to Sydney,' Cockburn said. He hung in the door of Inspector Bourke's office.

'How so?' Bourke was forced to ask. That was all the invitation Cockburn needed to come in and take a seat.

'Detective Sergeant Rochelle notified Travis Vella, the husband, yesterday. He's made himself scarce because the media's already on his doorstep. Now he's heading back to work, which at the moment is somewhere in the Victorian Mallee. I suppose if you want to hide, it'd be hard to beat the Mallee. She passed on his contact details for when we want to bring him in. It'll probably mean a trip to Mildura or Bendigo. There goes my chance to meet her in the flesh.'

He didn't hide his pleasure at saying "in the flesh".

'Give it a rest, Gary. She's probably married.'

'Your point being?'

Bourke shook his head despairingly and realised how quickly and inevitably he always reached this point with Cockburn. He pushed on.

'This all happened nearly five years ago, so tracking people's movements will be like trying to find a climate change enthusiast in the National Party. That doesn't mean I don't want you to try and try hard, but realistically, the only useful intel you'll be able to gather from back then is on the

New South Wales file. Have you made arrangements for access with Detective Sergeant Oglethorpe?'

He pointedly chose not to refer to her as Rochelle.

'She's happy to share the content but reluctant to physically part with everything.'

'Well, get on a plane to Sydney and check it out. I don't want you interviewing this character about stuff that happened five years ago without knowing every bit of hard evidence that's ever been placed on record.'

'So, you are happy for me to go and see Rochelle?' Cockburn beamed.

'Happy might not be the word I'd choose. Just prepare the paperwork, and I'll sign it. And one other thing. When you do the interview with Travis Vella, make sure Rory's there.'

'This is my case, right?' Cockburn said it slowly.

'You know how hard it is to read husbands who try and pull off shit like this. I want another pair of experienced eyes and ears sizing this bloke up. A second opinion if you like. You don't have to have Rory in the room so long as he's watching through the glass. Your case. Your call.

Chapter 13

'*Rory.*'

'Yeah. Is that you, Michelle?'

She'd spoken his name so softly into the phone that he wasn't immediately sure.

'*Can you come over?*' she murmured.

'Yeah, Sure. I thought you were in Sydney. I tried to call.'

'*Can you come round now?*' The voice was still soft, and the few extra words were enough to betray her just-holding-it-together-ness.

'Yep. Coming.' He looked at the clock on the wall. Eleven twenty PM.

Rory had chosen a post-marriage retreat in Elwood. The locale boasted its fair share of cool celebrities. Still, the only recognisable resident Rory had occasion to notice was Bridget

McKenzie. The ill-famed politician was ousted from the federal cabinet after the 2020 Sports Rorts scandal. He remembered being warned about some shonky types in the neighbourhood.

The beachside suburb with a mellow inner-city vibe chose Rory rather than the converse. His criteria of one-bedroom guaranteed a welcome departure from his former family-based addresses. Congestion, lack of parking and the exterior design of his 1960s cream-brick apartment block soon grated, but he remained for the coffee and nearness to St Kilda. Also, on the upside, the generous-sized rooms in his apartment were an irreplaceable relic of history, and he'd heard rumours that the building's unique ugliness was on the cusp of gaining it a heritage listing.

He abandoned a street-parking space he knew — even at midnight — would shortly disappear until fellow Elwood-ites began heading off to work in the pre-dawn darkness.

Michelle had also eschewed traditional suburban living for a new post-married-with-kids singles existence in the inner Melbourne village of Kensington. Her two-bedroom, two-storey duplex nestled uneasily among the Victoria terraces, cottages and warehouse apartments. Such intruders were not yet common nor presumably welcomed.

Rory was greeted by the same after-hours street-parking nightmare he'd come from. He wove through Kensington's grid of narrow streets and lanes until the headlights of someone else heading into the night blinked on. He pounced on the not-yet-cold park, locked his car and ran. Whether he'd be able to find his car again was not a consideration.

Michelle's doorbell button had the disconcerting habit of not confirming it had indeed activated a chime somewhere within the premises. Rory filled an interminable wait, trying to catch his breath. As he reached to press the button for the third time, a glow of soft light appeared behind the frosted glass window in Michelle's front door. It was soon eclipsed by a slowly approaching shape. The door opened.

Michelle stood in a dressing gown, looking tiny and defeated. She caught his eye just long enough to confirm it was him.

'I didn't think you'd come,' she sniffled with her head facing his chest.

He stepped in and wrapped his arms around her. He knew her emptiness. He knew he could do no more and no less than be with her. The embrace lasted so long he feared she might fall asleep.

'Let's lie you down,' he said.

Rory led her to the couch. A peace she hadn't known for days enveloped her with sleep. He found a doona, covered her, made himself a cup of tea, sat in the chair opposite, watched. He woke with a start at eight-thirty and went to the kitchen for another cup of tea. Phoned in sick. There was no need to offer a reason. No one wanted PTSD spelled out for them. The standing assumption was that he was having a bad day. If it lingered, he was having a bad week.

His reality was Michelle's reality. Swords of Damocles that hung above each of their lives, waiting for the next time the thread of horse-tail hair would snap unannounced, usually at night. Her lived experience of the same ever-present menace embodied the inimitable empathy that drew Rory to her. That gave Rory both solace and fear. The solace of someone who knew that avoiding it was false hope. The fear that such comfort may be the underlying attraction, rather than the person themselves. He was on his third cup of tea when she woke at eleven-thirty AM. She drew the hair off her face and smiled weakly.

'Are you drinking tea?' She eyed the wall clock. 'Haven't you had a coffee yet? You'll be getting the shakes if you're not careful.'

'It can wait,' he answered and gave her a considered look. 'You know, I knew this day would come, but I always thought it would be the other way round. I imagined it would be me in a heap, hopefully with you wondering why I went off the radar. I really thought that's how it would happen, not if it would happen. Then, when it did happen, and it was you that copped it, I didn't twig. I thought all the unanswered calls I'd made to you were because … I thought you were giving me the flick.'

'Yeah, well. That's not what I was dealing with. Not foremost.' She answered.

'I mean, you're the expert writing a book on the subject. In the back of my mind, I think I took it for granted that all your insight and wisdom would count for something. It didn't cross my mind that you'd ever let things get on top of you.'

'It's not by choice. Whoever wrote "physician, heal thyself" into the bible hadn't experienced PTSD. You know as well as anybody that when it strikes, you can't rely on logic or emotion. There's nothing you can take for granted. As far as affecting you and me, it left me feeling … I don't know … a life doubly-doomed to be fractured with episodes like this … what sort of future is that for a couple?'

'I'm just glad you did call me. That counts for something,' he said.

She sat up with the doona still around her.

'Come over here.'

He came over there and sat beside her. She tried to explain.

'You're right. You do count for something, and that's part of the problem. When the nightmares came this time, you were in them. That hasn't happened before. The nightmares I have about people I care about. The people I'm trying to protect in my dreams when everything goes to shit. The people I end up shutting out when this happens. That's where my mind ran … shutting you out. But don't worry. You may have made it into my nightmares, but for the right reasons. You know?'

He knew. He stretched his arm around her and pressed his lips onto the side of her face. She stared ahead and continued.

'I'm glad I got there in the end — I mean returning your call. I didn't end up going to Sydney. I bailed out of the conference without letting anyone know. I was already a mess because you know what you're in for. And you know you can't rise out of it until it plays out … whatever you try.' She made a point of not looking at the collection of empty bottles.

'I had other missed calls. I think they were from the conference organisers … but they didn't persist. So, thanks for coming round. I mean, really … thanks for coming round.'

Her eyes welled, and he turned his head slightly to place another soothing kiss on the side of her forehead. They both stared ahead in silence.

'... and somewhere in all that,' she announced, 'I remembered how good the sex was at Dunkeld.'

This time, he pulled his face back to look at her. He saw an ache to be kissed and obliged. It continued with increasing ardency until Michelle pulled back.

'I want to enjoy this, so why don't you pop down to the Kensington Premises and get us coffees. Let me have a shower first. I feel like shit — physically, I mean. It's been a couple of days.' Michelle said.

He leant back. They both smiled.

'I phoned in sick for the day, so the coffee can wait,' he said. 'But showering first sounds like a good idea. Let me help you.' They clamped back on to her just-woke-up kiss, flung off the doona, and staggered, kissed and undressed their way to the bathroom.

Chapter 14

Cockburn found himself deep within the bowels of the Sydney Police Centre — a brutalist-architecture fortress that made it onto some peoples' top-five ugliest buildings in the nation. Ugliness was not a thing with Rochelle Oglethorpe. The Detective Sergeant in her late thirties immediately surpassed the raven-haired goddess of Cockburn's imagination, a fantasy crushed just as swiftly by the cluster on her ring finger. Alongside the rock-laden engagement and wedding rings, a couple of other sterling bands had been added for good measure. It was unmistakably an underscored no-go reminder designed specifically for the uber-blokey world Rochelle navigated every working day.

Cockburn sighed.

'You okay?' she asked.

'The flight,' he sighed again.

The window in the small meeting room faced a nondescript corridor. No sign of the outside world. On the eight-seater table were several thick folders of documents and a laptop computer. Takeaway espresso coffees were delivered to the room. Cockburn nodded approvingly, slung his satchel onto the table and took a seat.

'I'd love to be investigating this,' Rochelle confessed unashamedly. 'It was me that did all the running first time round. Of course, we never had a body, so in the end, we had nowhere to go.'

Cockburn looked at her, not without a measure of scepticism.

'Shit happens,' he offered.

The experienced Detective Sergeant knew instantly what breed of cop she was dealing with.

'Okay then,' She pronounced in a so-that's-how-it-is way. 'What would you like to see first?'

Water ran off the duck's back.

'Mr Vella would be good. I presume you did a formal interview?'

'There's a video I can play to you now. You can take a copy on a USB stick and a photocopy of the written transcript.'

'Good. Well done,' he said patronisingly. 'Let's see what that looks like for a start.'

Rochelle dialled up the video on the laptop. A stark, harshly lit interview room appeared. Travis Vella sat with his forearms on the small tabletop, opposite the back of Rochelle's head. His older, male legal counsel to his left. Another police officer was out of shot to Rochelle's right. The digital date stamp and timer flickered in the corner. The laptop audio was thin as they listened to Rochelle spell out the interview preliminaries.

'What are the interesting bits?' Cockburn asked.

Rochelle pressed pause and took a breath.

'For me, when we asked him if he had returned to Sydney on the day she disappeared was interesting.'

'Can we fast forward to look at that then?'

Cockburn took the plastic lid off his coffee while Rochelle began navigating the video.

'This is cappuccino. Have you got mine?'

'No. Mine's black. I thought you told Mandy you have it white.'

'Yeah, but I thought she was doing instant. It's all right. This'll do then.'

Rochelle held her gaze on him an extra beat before she resumed searching the video.

'Here you go,' she said, then listened and cringed as her own voice seemed to squawk out of the laptop's tiny invisible speakers:

'You said you were in Victoria on the weekend that Gloria disappeared. You didn't happen to return to Sydney during any of that period, did you?'

'I've been waiting for this. You lot are as bad as the media. You're letting them lead you rather than getting down to some proper policing. What about fingerprints, DNA, CCTV, whatever it is you do these days?'

'Do you mind answering the question for the record, Mr Vella? Did you return to Sydney on the weekend of your wife's disappearance?'

'Of course, I bloody didn't. Do you know how long it would take to drive to Sydney and back?'

'We do know how long it takes to drive to Sydney and back. It takes eleven hours each way. That's one day and one night, which is how long your whereabouts can't be vouched for by the caravan park operator where you stayed in Balmoral.'

'Well, how would they know? They'd be the first to tell you they are not my keeper. I was in an on-site cabin with an en-suite. They're usually busy in their café, and they don't have a line of sight to the cabin, let alone my vehicle, which is usually parked on the other side. The place is not that busy, but they have other guests. Did you ask any of them?'

'Enough of them,' Rochelle said. 'Can you tell me why you stay in the caravan park and not the hotel?'

'I've stayed there before, it's fine. It's not like the pub is five-star. I think they only charge about sixty bucks a night. Look, I always work on the weekends I'm away ... to maximise my time there. I've given you the location of the properties I visited for my work. Have you asked around there?'

'As much as the Victorian police could. Those areas were all rural and sparsely populated. And you didn't have Tony, your surveying assistant, to hold the staff or whatever he does, so he can't verify that you were where you said. And out of interest, how do you survey without someone holding the staff?'

'Of course, Tony can't tell you he saw me there. He's a local, and he has the weekend off, which doesn't mean I can't do other stuff, like selecting sites, photographing features, mapping, paperwork.'

'So you're saying you didn't return to Sydney on the weekend Gloria went missing,'

'No.'

On the video, Travis harrumphed and folded his arms. Rochelle clicked pause. Cockburn cut loose.

'Whoa. There's a guilty man right there. It sounds like he thought the whole thing through. "No line of sight" at the caravan park, his offsider Tony conveniently not there. He's not at the pub because they would probably see him and his vehicle come and go.'

'Yeah, well hold that thought, Columbo, it continues.' Rochelle clicked Play again.

'Okay. You say you didn't return to Sydney. So, can you tell us why no calls were made on your mobile phone all day Saturday? It appears to have been turned off.'

The video appears to pause, but it was Travis wondering how to answer the question. He turned to his counsel, who gave him a grave but knowing nod.

'Alright. I was with a woman. Her name is Carol Warren. She lives on a farm south of there. I stayed at her place on Friday night. I had my phone turned off until I was back in Balmoral on Saturday. I didn't want to be interrupted, especially by Gloria. By Saturday evening, when I began trying to phone Gloria, I realised my phone was still switched off. I didn't tell you before because I didn't want Carol to be involved — not since the media latched on. I was a thousand kilometres from Sydney, so I didn't think I needed an alibi. I didn't think it would matter one iota how I had spent my time in Victoria. Nor did I think people who could vouch for me would be short on the ground.'

'Did Gloria know about your affair?'

He kept his gaze lowered as he spoke.

'She did know ... just. It erupted a couple of days before my trip to Victoria ... a lead balloon, of course. At that stage, we didn't get beyond shouting at each other and mega-brooding. We both knew it was over, but Gloria was too angry to talk about how we would go about separating. That's why I had my phone switched off the night I stayed with Carol. A call from an ex-in-waiting is a mood killer, even if you don't answer it.'

Rochelle hit Pause again.

'That's how it unfolded before our eyes,' she told Cockburn.

'So, if he did it, this Carol is covering for him?'

The suggestion that Travis Vella killed his wife sounded novel to Rochelle.

'If he did it?' she answered.

138

Cockburn answered with equal incredulity.

'What? After all that … and now with her body laid squarely at his feet, you think that somehow it's not him?'

'I have to admit that's where I would have placed my money before the body was discovered. Now, I'm having doubts.'

Cockburn unleashed:

'Having doubts? Am I missing something? Married man finds himself a newer model. His wife finds out and cracks it. The next thing you know, she goes missing. Nothing to do with him, of course; he's working interstate. Four and a half years later, she's dug up a thousand kilometres away, at the exact place the husband clings to as his interstate alibi. Her body is found under six metres of dirt that was never going to be dug up again, ever, something a geologist working in the area would know well. And by the way, that six metres of dirt still hasn't been dug up again; that's how unlucky he was.

'So much for the alibi of being a thousand miles away. The question then became: did he have an opportunity to pop back to Sydney? You … the New South Wales police force … tell him he did have a window that no one can account for. You get him with his back against the wall, and lo and behold, he brings the never-before-mentioned mistress in on the act. Yeah right.

'Still, in your defence, I suppose it all seemed a bit academic without knowing what actually happened to her. Now you have a body. I mean, we do — Victoria Police. I'm gonna enjoy seeing what he tries to pull out of the hat to explain that away.'

She looked at him with a pained expression.

'What? Don't tell me you ....'

She cut him off.

'Don't you dare accuse me of women's intuition.'

'I was going to say, hunch,' he answered truthfully. Nonetheless, this time it didn't run off the duck's back. It had sunk in that they sat on opposite sides.

'And I was going to say, motive,' she responded. 'What motive would he have to kill her? They didn't have kids. He was leaving her; she wasn't leaving him for someone else. Their house was three parts mortgaged. If they did separate, no one was going to walk away with a big financial advantage. Not even with the best of lawyers.'

Cockburn was quick to put it back on her.

'You tell me? It was your case. How bad was the relationship? Sometimes it doesn't take much,' Cockburn countered.

She thought about his question but took another line when she answered.

'It was me who told him his wife's body had been found. He still lives in the same house in East Hills. He and Carol now have two children. I have to say he was very convincing at being totally dismayed about where Gloria was found. That was the thing that shook him most. The first place his mind went after that was, someone did an excellent job of aiming this squarely at him.'

'Not evidence, though, is it? Did you ask him who he thought would do that to him?'

'It wasn't my case, and I didn't want to prejudice how you want to go about it. I was simply there to inform the next of kin that his wife was dead.'

'Sure.'

'Well, it's your case now. It's all in there.' She nodded to the pile of lever arch files.

'Take as long as you like. I've booked the room for the whole day. There's a photocopier next door. Copy what you need.

'What I will say before I go is, we did ask him about anyone who might have it in for him or his wife. There were a few people he'd locked horns with in his job. None close to home, though, and none that amounted to serious suspects. It's all in there, but you might want to revisit that in light of where her body was found. We also worked hard on the window he had to travel back to Sydney. Checked CCTV on roads and at roadhouses, his credit card use, etcetera. Came up with nothing. There were also a couple of houses in the neighbourhood with CCTV. That's all in there too.'

Cockburn's face fell at the prospect of how the rest of his day in the harbour city would be spent. Rochelle couldn't resist a wicked parting shot.

'The only thing I can't vouch for is how well the net was cast for witnesses around Balmoral who could have backed his alibi. That was done by Vic police. I know it was nearly five years ago, but you wouldn't want Travis Vella finding someone your boys missed.'

And she deliberately said "boys".

Chapter 15

Tahlia parked the Parks Victoria four-wheel drive at the Anderson Creek crossing and walked the final kilometre to the gemstone site. A decaying but official fossicking reserve signboard sprang up well before the actual diggings appeared. A predominance of tall, smooth-barked yellow gums created a parkland below the dense stringy bark scrub along the ridge. Groundcover was a carpet of kangaroo-trimmed grass and a smattering of tiny red Trailing Hop-bush flowers. The world's largest remaining population — a mere 1,000 specimens of the poorly-known and threatened species — was on the wane. Nonetheless, it was a second rare gem occupying the same skerrick of bush. What were the odds?

Terry's caravan soon appeared on the brow of the rise. Once again, he had the gem site to himself. Forensics, media and rubberneckers had all decamped to the next tragedy.

Cockatoos kicked up a stink as Tahlia approached. That set kookaburras off in the bush beyond. It also alerted Terry's companion. She rose from her deluxe camping chair under the annex and circled the van. Tahlia found herself facing an Aboriginal woman. A woman who'd passed into middle age. Her hair was still black, falling in a thick fan of tight waves.

'You're back. Haven't got your copper mate with you this time?'

'Nah. I thought he might spook you again. That's also why I walked in.'

'He didn't spook me. Just that I don't talk to cops if I don't have to. Or anyone in uniform,' she added, casting an eye at Tahlia's Parks Victoria outfit.

'Don't blame you,' Tahlia said convincingly.

Terry's companion gave an apologetic shrug.

'Where you from?' Tahlia asked.

'Narungga woman.'

'South Australian?'

'Yeah. That's where Terry's from too. How'd you know?'

'Aboriginal studies. Part of doing archaeology at uni … and the van's number plate is South Australian.'

She smiled. You wanna cuppa tea? I was about to put the billy on.'

'Yeah, thanks.'

'Rose is my name, by the way.'

'Tahlia.'

'Yeah. I know. Terry told me. It's a pretty name.'

Terry was busy laying out cables to harness an earth-moving scoop to his ute. The scoop was positioned to begin dragging loads of mullock back into the shaft he'd spent the past couple of months sinking by hand. At least for this part of the process, he had gravity on his side. He crawled out from under the back of his ute, more dust-encrusted than when he'd toiled in the shaft. His shorts were on their last legs … so to speak.

He shielded his eyes to see who was with Rose. He didn't need time to sum up the situation. Gave a wave and a "Hi Tahlia" and was back under the other side of the ute.

'He's hoping he can get the hole filled tomorrow so we can head off on Friday,' Rose said.

'Does he need you helping him?'

'I will when he has everything hitched up. I do the driving. He guides the scoop.'

They fell into silence as Rose made the tea on the gas camp stove and produced a packet of biscuits. It was a comfortable silence. Once settled with their teas, Rose asked:

'Why'd you come back 'ere?'

'I wanted to see you. I thought you might be from the local mob and know about this place. No one else I spoke to does.'

Rose nodded and sipped her tea. She watched how Terry was doing.

'So, there's nothing you can tell me?' Tahlia persisted.

'No. I never met anyone from the local mob. Maybe they didn't know about it either. Before the white fellas, this little patch of bush wouldn't have looked no different from that bit over there.'

She pointed randomly, and they dropped back into tea-drinking silence to think about it.

'Something I do know though. When Terry found that woman's body, the first thing I felt was a black spirit. I really thought she was gonna be black. That's before they unwrapped her and found out she was white, I mean.

'When you showed up with that copper, I thought it musta had something to do with you. You had that look about you … not settled … like now, I suppose. But when they found out that woman was white, nothing changed. I still felt a black spirit. That's a presence I didn't mistake. It was strong.'

Terry stood. Tested the cables' grip by hand. He turned to Rose.

'You right to give it a burl, luv?'

It was time for Tahlia to leave.

'Thanks, Rose. That's what I came to hear.'

'Hang on. Before you go. Have this.'

She reached into a pocket and retrieved a modest-sized smoky quartz crystal.

'Not the biggest one you'll find … or the best cut. But this one has an energy. I think you'll need it more than me.'

Back at the car, she checked for a mobile phone signal. One bar. It might be enough to get the job done. She leaned against the car and dialled.

'*Detective Sergeant Rory James,*' Rory answered.

'It's Tahlia.'

'*Hi. I've been meaning to call you. I spoke to Leona Craig, one of Ricky's mates on his Halls Gap trip. Hang on while I get my notes out.*'

'So, you have had a look at Ricky's case? I was just ringing to see.'

Rory detected surprise in her voice. He'd earned brownie points at the first hurdle. That was good.

'*Yes, I have. Leona mentioned an Indigenous bloke named Leonard Dalton. He was a local who showed them around the traps. Do you know him, and can you get me his details?*'

'I know of Lenny. I'll find out his details and text them. Did Leona tell you anything else?'

'*She said Ricky latched onto separate interests while they were there. That's why he wasn't with Leona and Lucas when he went missing. Ricky went off chasing some of the post-European local history stuff, including a massacre. Did you know about any of this?*'

'No. Not at all. At that stage, I hadn't started uni. Ricky's studies would have meant nothing to me.'

'*That's okay. I'll speak to Lenny and see what he can tell me. I also want to talk to the kid who survived the accident in Ricky's car. You said you spoke to him and you were going to send me his details. Did you forget or couldn't you find them?*'

'Sorry. I had a mobile phone number for him, but it's not connected anymore. I'll try Facebook or something. Like I did the first time I tracked him down.'

'*His name is on the accident file, but there's no contact details, probably because he wasn't the driver. The name I've got is Ethan Hall. Is that right?*'

'Yeah. That's him.'

'Alright. Let me know when you find him. In the meantime, I'll catch up on other stuff that should have been followed through at the time. There's still a lot of legwork to do, I'm afraid.'

'I've got time,' she said before they bade their phone farewells.

Tahlia held her phone to her chest reassuringly and looked at a red-necked wallaby watching from a safe distance.

'"Not settled", Rose reckons. We'll see about that,' she told the wallaby.

Chapter 16

'How fucking convenient is this trip to Bendigo for you? An all-expenses paid excuse to shag Sigrid Dobell. Well, I'm driving straight back to Melbourne after we interview Vella. Don't expect me to cool my heels in Bendigo while you indulge in some afternoon delight. You want to spear the bearded clam, then you can catch the train back.'

Rory winced.

'I'm not seeing her anymore,' he told Cockburn.

Cockburn took his eyes off the road to look at Rory in the passenger seat.

'She gave you the flick?'

Rory shook his head.

'So, she did give you the flick,' Cockburn crowed.

'None of your fucking business,' Rory snapped, which in Cockburn's mind translated literally to mean "Yes. I admit it".

'She gave you the flick.' Cockburn concluded again.

Rory wanted to shake his head again but needed to break the circle.

'How did you go with Rochelle?'

Glee drained from Cockburn's face. He recovered just as quickly.

'Great. She handed me the Travis Vella case, all tied up with a pretty bow. I think she was shitty that he buried the body in Victoria. Not in New South Wales. It's all there in the files on the back seat. His affair, his fucked alibi — his bit-on-the-side covering for him. All that was missing was a body … until now. Our body, our case, our win … handed to us on a platter.'

Rory read between the lines.

'So, you didn't hit it off?'

'She was bitter … and as married as.'

That told Rory exactly how the inter-force cooperative investigation played out. Exactly as he expected it would.

'How are you going to play it today?'

'Walk him through it, from start to finish. See how he tries to explain everything away. See if there are any holes we need to plug, which there won't be. This is a no brainer. We don't need any good cop bad cop cuteness. It's my lead; you're the observer. Practice being the strong silent type. Okay?'

'Where is he working?'

'I dunno. Somewhere in the Mallee. It was a choice of interviewing him in Bendigo or Mildura. I know you love my company, but I didn't think you'd fancy an extra eight hours in the car. So, Bendigo it is.'

'Don't be so hard on yourself. You show great perception.'

Cockburn eyed him suspiciously. Rory jumped in again before Cockburn figured out the backhander.

'What do they mine in the Mallee? Did he say?'

'What's that got to do with it? Mallee roots, bulls, dust — I dunno.'

Rory tried not to sigh too pointedly and grabbed the file to read.

Travis Vella arrived in his high-viz work attire. Rory wondered if that was a strategic decision by his Sydney lawyer, Lincoln Renfrey. It was obvious that dress was no accidental matter for Lincoln. He, too, wore his everyday outfit. In his case, a lustrous suit with a pattern in the weave. A pattern so subtle you found yourself looking a third time, just to be sure it was actually there. His blue shirt played a trick of its own. It was so pale, it left you wondering if it was, in fact, a white shirt basking in blue ness reflected by the silk tie. Expensive fabrics have a way of not going unnoticed.

Why would Lincoln bother about what Travis Vella wore? Rory contemplated. There was no judge or jury to influence here, not unless the interview, which would be videoed, eventually made it into court as evidence. Even in that event, did high-vis down-to-earthiness offer any advantage? Perhaps Lincoln knew how people thought better than they did themselves.

Rory did the honours of greeting Travis and Lincoln in the reception space at Bendigo Police Station and ushered them to an interview room.

'Thanks for coming in,' he greeted them.

Although the three men were roughly the same age, Lincoln stood out. Better dressed, to begin with, he sported a black beard rather than the clean shaven-ness of Rory and Travis, his closely cropped short hair was just long enough to part and comb. He was also a couple of centimetres taller than the other two, something accentuated by a countenance of appearing to look down on others.

Cockburn sat as soon as he was introduced. Rory, Travis and Lincoln poured themselves water from the glass pitcher. Cockburn waited. He was oblivious to his own knee jiggling up and down … as Lincoln was not.

'Right,' Lincoln announced himself ready before Cockburn could take charge. Cockburn knew.

'I presume you are registered to practice law in Victoria,' Cockburn said, purely to wrestle the perceived upper hand back.

'Detective Sergeant, please give me credit for knowing a little about the law, and I won't ask you to produce your own bona fides.'

'I've had Sydney lawyers waltz across the Murray River and think they can automatically throw their weight around,' Cockburn dug in.

'If you say so, Detective Sergeant, but if you want to go further down this road, I'd like you to turn the tape on now, please.'

'I'll take that as a yes; you are registered to practice in Victoria,' Cockburn said and smiled needlessly.

'So, can we get on with it then,' Lincoln said.

Great start, Gary, Rory observed in his head.

Cockburn shifted his stare from Lincoln.

'Mr Vella. I'm sorry about the death of your wife … Gloria.' Cockburn loaded the statement with a deliberate delay before he added "Gloria".

The innuendo was that Travis had put the matter so far behind himself that he needed to be reminded of the name of his missing wife. Travis inhaled audibly through his nose and remained silent. He looked at Lincoln and silently acknowledged they were both in for a combative interrogation.

Rory fired up the recording equipment and cited the formalities of naming those present, time, date, place, etcetera. Rory's comparatively amiable demeanour was not lost on Travis Vella or Lincoln Wallace. Was he deliberately being the good cop? Cockburn took the running.

'Mr Vella, ten days ago, your wife's body was found over six metres below ground level at the bottom of a mine shaft that had been completely re-filled. The mineshaft is located on the Mooralla Gemstone Reserve that we believe you may have become familiar with in the process of undertaking mineral exploration in the area as part of your employment.

'A post mortem was carried out on the remains of your wife. The pathologist believes the body has been buried from about the time your wife went missing over four years ago. The post mortem reveals that more than likely, your wife died of asphyxia, probably as a result of environmental suffocation. The post mortem also revealed your wife suffered a blow to the head in the time leading up to when she suffocated. More than likely, the blow to the head was not in itself fatal.'

Cockburn paused for a reaction. Travis Vella's face had paused with the shock of what he was hearing. He was the first to speak.

'Environmental suffocation. What's that? Does it mean she was buried alive?'

Cockburn wasn't ready for the question. Rory answered.

'Environmental suffocation means she was somewhere, probably in a confined space, where the oxygen ran out. Although her remains are four and a half years old, the depth at which she was buried slowed decomposition enough for the pathologist to be able to rule out being buried alive and to rule out choking or smothering. However, the pathologist was unable to determine exactly what circumstances caused your wife's suffocation. I'm sorry, Mr Vella.'

Rory's sincerity fell beyond any "good-cop" routine, if not rivalling a Morgan Freeman performance.

'Jesus. When they told me she died of asphyxia, I thought she had been strangled. I don't know what's worse,' Travis Vella said and dropped his head. Lincoln placed a hand on his shoulder.

Cockburn looked from Rory to Travis Vella to Lincoln and then jumped in.

'You know what strikes me about the circumstances I just described?' Cockburn said, intending the question to be rhetorical.

'That there are enough convenient circumstances for you to ignore the possibility that my client was not involved.' Lincoln answered.

'Half right. Not bad for a Sydney-sider,' Cockburn shot back.

'I take it that you have accessed New South Wales records from Gloria's disappearance, and you know that my client has accounted for his presence in Victoria at the time his wife went missing. And as far as I know, an alibi is an alibi, even under Victorian law.'

'You mean getting his bit-on-the-side to alibi him?'

Cockburn turned from Lincoln to Travis Vella to continue.

'Until the New South Wales police revealed to you that no one in the area you said you were in could vouch for your whereabouts, you insisted you spent the time doing work stuff … alone. It was only when that story was brought into question by the lack of mobile phone usage that you came up with an alibi from …' Cockburn opened the manila folder to read the name. '… Carol Warren. Why did you lie?'

Travis Vella glared his answer.

'Carol is not "a bit-on-the-side". Carol is my life partner, and we now have two children. You refer to her as that again, and I'm going to walk right out of here … and be grateful that that's all I do. And I didn't lie. Carol was my business, and I didn't want her to become involved in any way. Unless I had good reason to do otherwise, I was leaving her out of the picture to protect her.'

'Threatening a police officer. On camera …'

Lincoln grabbed Travis Vella's shoulder. His grip told Travis to let him respond.

'If you play back the recording of this meeting, you will clearly hear my client making the point that he will do nothing more than walk out of here if he is provoked in that way again. I insist that the exchange does not get deleted or edited in any way.'

When spoken by a lawyer, there were more than enough connotations in those two sentences to sound exactly like a threat, one that caused Cockburn to think instead of talk. It allowed Lincoln to continue.

'I can assure you Carol Warren is not about to alter her statement or perjure herself in any way to suit a theory that may have already been concocted by you. Travis has come here today to do whatever he can to help you find whoever committed this crime. He wants you to pursue the case vigorously, and he wants to help. Are there any such questions you'd like to ask him?'

Somehow it had become Lincoln's interview. Cockburn wasn't about to play ball.

Rory spoke before Cockburn could come up with his next salvo.

'Can I put this a different way? I understand from the New South Wales missing persons record that, at that time, your relationship with Carol Warren was at an early stage. In the New South Wales interview, you also mentioned you didn't want the media latching onto Carol. Can you tell us what Carol's situation was at the time? Was she also married, or was there anything else in particular that media exposure would aggravate … any more than usual?'

It seems it was an anticipated question. Lincoln nodded to Travis Vella to explain.

'Carol owned a farm near where I was working in Victoria. I first went there to negotiate access to do some exploration work. That's how we met. She had been widowed … not that long beforehand, to be frank. Our getting together would have been too soon as far as her brother-in-law, and her father-in-law were concerned. They had already shown their true colours by contesting Nigel's estate. Nigel was Carol's husband. He died of cancer without a will, and financially, Nigel's property was intertwined in the wider family enterprise. In their eyes, Carol was a ring-in who wasn't entitled to any of it, despite her automatic entitlement as next of kin. Having a new partner on the scene had the potential to compromise those financial challenges Carol was defending, which were not insubstantial. If her father-in-law and brother-in-law got wind of me being in the scene, they would have tried to use that against her in the legal battle. In fact, they did exactly that after Carol was named in the media. In the end, the farm did pass back to the family, but not without Carol gaining her fair entitlement.'

'So, you were keen to keep the relationship under wraps,' Rory summed up Travis's account.

'When it began, we always met at her farm. We never went into town. She would also turn her phone off when we spent time together. So, you see, the last thing Carol needed on her plate was to become part of a public circus she had no direct involvement in. You also have to remember that we never knew for sure that Gloria was dead. At that stage, how I spent my private time in Victoria was academic to the case. In the end, I did need Carol to vouch for me, and she didn't hesitate.'

'Well, let *me* put it a different way,' Cockburn said. 'You're trying to talk up her credibility and your own credibility with a story about covertly scheming together in a financial battle against her in-laws.'

'Responding strategically … in a battle neither my client nor his partner sought, may I remind you, Detective Sergeant,' Lincoln answered. 'And as a detective, it shouldn't go unnoticed that, for their own perfidious reasons, there are others who don't think well of my client. People who well might have wanted to harm him or his family, as it was then. I hope you are not leaving stones un-turned in your investigation.'

Cockburn didn't know what perfidious meant, but he wasn't having a bar of it.

'Then tell me. If such people exist, why would they kill Mr Vella's wife in Sydney, transport her body all the way to where Mr Vella was working in Victoria, bury her under six metres of soil, six metres mind you, of spent mining soil? That's soil that no one on the planet will ever find a reason to dig up again. That's a fucking long way to go to dump a body you don't want to be found … unless you just happen to be in the neighbourhood. And whoever it was, they certainly weren't planning for it to be found and thereby implicate your client.' Silence fell as answers went begging. Cockburn glowed triumphantly.

Chapter 17

'Foehckin 'ell, is that what I've been asking people about?'

The accent was excitable-Irish. It had a habit of slipping out whenever Detective Natalie O'Quinn was moved to exclaim. In this instance, she had her nose to the crime board, peering down Terry's mineshaft in a photograph she'd just finished attaching to the board. The rectangle of earthen walls tapered to unfathomable gloom. Along one side, an extension ladder reached the shaky mid-shaft platform. Another ladder beyond that disappeared into the murk.

The subterranean scene was last in a row of four photographs that otherwise included individual portrait shots of Carol Warren and Travis Vella and one of the blue tarp with Gloria Travis still wrapped inside.

As well as assembling the crime board, Natalie had the task of tracking down the gem-site's infrequent visitors and any intelligence about deep shafts that were dug four or five years earlier.

She turned to Cockburn to explain herself.

'I've seen the place on news footage and all that, but I didn't imagine they were diggin' their way to China. That's one deep hole for any man to dig with a pick and shovel.'

'It's where they get the really good stuff,' Cockburn said in normal speak.

His new offsider had only recently migrated to Australia and replaced Detective Julia O'Hannagain, whom Cockburn had begun, and subsequently ended, a relationship with. Julia — who was also of Irish stock, albeit second generation — was sacked for passing on privileged information. The parallels spooked Cockburn into being on his best behaviour. He kept his sailing-close-to-the-wind repartee holstered when Natalie was around. Rory enjoyed Cockburn's internal battle of self-restraint as he and Cockburn watched her straighten the photos. *It won't last*, he concluded.

Bourke arrived for his briefing. Natalie, Rory and Cockburn stood back and watched him take in the four photos on the crime board. Nothing else had been added.

'So that's Travis Vella?' he began. Then turned to Cockburn.

'How'd you go with him, Gary?'

'He's our man as far as I'm concerned. He's got no alibi unless you count the bit-of-fluff he was shagging on the side vouching for him. But he only arranged for her to do that after the New South coppers had his back against the wall.'

'I think you mean he's got an alibi unless his current life partner was to unaccountably rescind her statement,' Rory said.

'That's not out of the question. Vella as good as admitted to us that her previous in-laws regard her as a piece of work. Her husband died of cancer, and the way Vella described it himself, she well and truly got her claws into the family farm. We're yet to chase any of that down, but I'd be surprised if we don't find something we can use to turn the heat on her.'

'I gather that's not the way you see it, Rory?' Bourke asked.

'The alibi thing bothers me for the opposite reason. I read the New South Wales file. Vella was hesitant at first, trying to keep his girlfriend out of it, but the New South cops didn't seem overly concerned about the alibi in any case. I think that was because it was still a missing person investigation at that stage. They weren't dealing with a murder. And the idea of Vella driving up to Sydney and back seemed a hell of a stretch. It still is. It was so fucking far with such a small window of opportunity. As far as doing their own checks on his whereabouts, it probably didn't help that they were at arm's length. Much of what they relied on was done by Vic police.'

'So, what are you saying? We did a shit job?' Bourke asked.

'Who knows how committed our troops were to a person gone missing in Sydney. I'm just saying, be careful about locking in any assumption. You wouldn't want to be ambushed in court if their defence team shows up with a swag of local witnesses who remember seeing him around the place, even after four years. It's the country and country people remember who they see. There's not many of them about out in the paddocks. Having said that, it's hard to see how it could be someone else who killed her and buried the body where they did.'

Cockburn gave an I-told-you-so grin.

'What about the gemstone site? What have you unearthed there, Natalie?'

'Jesus, your jokes are as bad as me dad's.'

She referred to her notes to continue.

'The good news is, not that many really deep shafts get dug. By the sound of it, there are some years when none at all are dug. The bad news is, I can confirm everything you've heard so far about trying to track down who actually dug them, where they dug them, and when. Fellas that no other fossickers have ever heard of might blow in and blow out and, depending on timing, no one knows they've ever been there. Not because they try to fly under the radar. It just so happens that no one else might go near the place for weeks on end. No one keeps a record of who comes or who goes, and no one seems to monitor or police what goes on.

'The whole place is off the radar if you ask me. That bit of bush is supposedly in Parks Victoria's bailiwick, but it doesn't crack a mention on their website. The gemstone site itself is also pretty invisible when it comes to local tourism. You're struggling to find mention of it in any brochure or website. Seems to me to be a really specialised thing. The funny thing is, though, is how at odds that is with all the online stuff about the Mooralla smoky quartz crystals themselves. It's massive. So, someone must be going there.'

Natalie turned the page in her notes.

'The gem collectors' club in Horsham have had a bit to do with the site since it started, although it seems they don't have any formal stewardship of the place. Nor do they keep records of who digs what, where or when. However, I was told it was them that installed the long-drop toilets there back in the eighties … and remind me to hold on if I ever go there. Apparently, when you lift the toilet seat, the number of blowflies that are unleashed sounds like a jumbo jet taking off.

'What I also learnt was, the requirement to fill your hole in before you leave is not always observed. One fella thought the park managers brought machinery in to do that from time to time. Someone else thought a local fella did it.'

'That's right,' Rory chipped in. 'His name is Hal Rogers. I've got his contact details. The story I was told about him is, he's a local landowner that one old fossicker prevailed upon to get his front-end-loader out and fill his hole in.'

Rory recognised a Cockburn-devour-able multi-entendre only as he voiced it. Cockburn not so much as sniggered. *It must be killing him*, Rory perceived before the moment passed. At least Bourke and Natalie cocked an eyebrow. Natalie continued.

'I'll give him a call, but this is shaping up as a hopeless task. The only hole I know of that was definitely sunk was a fella who says he went down about four metres four years ago. When I asked him if he could pinpoint the location, he said he thought it was somewhere on the uphill half of the diggings, and probably closer to the right-hand side than the left … when you're facing uphill. That's what we're up against. Everyone knows someone else who might know someone who knows something. I'm also trying to make contact with an American fella with a website. There's a photograph of his hole on the webpage.'

She paused in acknowledgement of the smirks.

'He makes the trip every couple of years. He refers to it as rockhounding. There's no scarcity of rabbit burrows to keep going down.'

'Thanks, Natalie, and keep on it. We can't leave any stones unturned.'

The other three all groaned.

'Fuck off. I didn't mean that one. It just slipped out. And get onto this Hal Rogers and the park's managers. They sound like our best bet. One of them probably filled the hole Gloria Vella was found in without even knowing somebody had already chucked her body in there and covered it with a few shovelfuls of dirt.'

'Will do, boss.'

'What about you, Rory? Have you done anything about our Indigenous consultant's missing brother? Have you saved us from being a podcast yet?'

'The short answers are yes and yes. I dug out the file, and I can confirm that the case was way under-investigated … and for all the wrong reasons. So, at least we've stopped that timebomb from ticking. I've started speaking to his mates to get a handle on what he was up to before he went missing and where he might have been heading. I reckon there's a trail of sorts. All the same, it's hard to be hopeful of a good result after so long. But who knows? Early days.'

'Okay. You stick with that, Rory. Gary and Natalie can double down on the Gloria Vella stuff. And Gary, why don't you send Natalie to wherever Travis Vella was hanging out to re-check his alibi movements … and get some names and a few arrows on this crime board. Next time I'm here, I want to know who's who, and I want it to tell me a story.'

Chapter 18

'Before I tempt you with a kangaroo steak sanga or emu sausage, let me show you around.'

Rory sensed Lenny Dalton would not be averse to taking the piss with a bit of blackfella humour. Lenny had suggested they meet at the Brambuk National Park and Cultural Centre at Halls Gap. Rory did his online homework to discover the unique complex began life as a flagship venue for the various Grampians Aboriginal communities. The site was later extended to serve as the general Grampians National Park information centre as well as maintaining its traditional cultural information role. A brief raison d'etre on the website referred to Brambuk as a symbol of renewal after Aboriginal dispossession and resistance. It proudly claimed one hundred percent Aboriginal ownership and operation.

That pride was evident in Lenny's bearing as he strode toward Rory across the carpark. The tall, near forty-year-old with a close-cropped black beard could nearly pass as a thicker-set version of Adam Goodes. His reference to emu sausage related to the centre's Bushfoods Café.

'I'm keen to do both. I read the café's Tripadvisor reviews. Four stars,' Rory answered.

His gaze shifted from Lenny in a vain search for the iconic Brambuk building he'd become familiar with online. Lenny noticed.

'The original building's around the back. This entry building is more recent.'

He gestured to a comparatively nondescript building with a large glass entrance. The Mount William range behind it made it appear lower than it probably was.

'I'll take you there first. Follow me.'

They skirted the entry building until the vast earthy-coloured roof of the original Brambuk masterpiece came into view. The rolling undulations of corrugated iron appeared to have mushroomed from the very foothills the building sat in.

'I read that the mindboggling roof is representative of the range behind it or of a cockatoo in flight. Now that I'm here, it also reminds me of the dune-like roof on Southern Cross station in Melbourne. It's also a lot like the centre I saw when I visited Uluru. Do you know the one I mean?'

'Oh yeah. I get all that. But it's not only the roof that's symbolic. The curved ramp inside represents eels. Even the building materials provide connections to our surrounding past — mud bricks as used on the mission at Antwerp, stonework represents pre-European stone houses and fish traps at Lake Condah. Stuff like that. And the reason it reminds you of the Uluru centre is, the architect Greg Burgess also did that one — but only after he pioneered the concept here. You're looking at the original.'

Lenny proceeded to give Rory a guided tour within. He cheerily greeted a couple of employees, showing a bus group around.

'Do you work here?' Rory asked.

'Nah. But I used to. I work for myself these days. Private tours. Stuff like that.'

Rory nodded, then made an observation.

'I reckon these columns made of unmilled tree trunks add a bit of the Murtoa stick-shed feel to the inside. You know, the massive 1940s wheat storage they call the Cathedral of the Wimmera? It's another famous attraction up this way, isn't it?'

Lenny frowned scornfully.

'Yeah, I know the place. It's nothing like this. I think we need to get a bit of bush tucker into you to calm you down. C'mon.'

A revelation met Rory when they exited the original Brambuk. He faced the rear of the hitherto nondescript entry building. From this angle, it transformed into a worthy architectural creation in its own right. Its fresher and crisper design referenced an Aboriginal eel trap, and the tall glass facade was oriented for maximum appreciation of the mountains' dominating presence. To the right, al fresco umbrellas sprouted outside the Bush Foods café. Rory and Lenny chose an outdoor table.

Lenny insisted on sharing the bushfoods platter — intent on Rory having a taste of everything. Rory insisted on a long black to go with it. With orders placed, only the main order of business remained to be dealt with. Lenny obliged.

'So, Ricky Lock? I take it he still hasn't shown up?'

'No, he hasn't. And it looks like this will be your first say on the matter. There's no record on the file of my colleagues speaking to you when he went missing.'

'That'd be right.'

'What makes you say it like that? Do you think there was stuff at play about him being Aboriginal, or you being Aboriginal?'

Lenny crossed his arms, dropped his head and shook it for some seconds. He took a deep breath before lifting his gaze to answer.

'Nah, man. I mean, the cops mighta been like that, I dunno. I would have been happy to talk to them, but they never asked me. If they did, I'd have nothing to tell them anyway. As I understand it, Leona and Lucas didn't report him missing for a few days after the event. I never knew anything about it until I ran into 'em well after that. I would have been well down the chain of the last people to see him.'

'Hmm.'

'What? You don't believe me?'

'Of course, I believe you. It's just that the more I look into this, the more missed opportunities I come across.'

'What does that mean?'

'Tell me if I'm wrong, but until Ricky went missing, you were the person he was spending most of his time with.'

'Yeah, but I wasn't with him every day or anything … and we were just doing normal stuff … or normal stuff that a guide

showing an archaeologist around does. He always headed
back to the hostel each night. If he was involved in anything
else or ran into any trouble, it was nothing I knew anything
about.'

'What about the massacre site Leona Craig told me you
took them to?'

'What about it? I took them to heaps of cultural sites. That
was my job. And anyway, the massacre site doesn't exist. I
mean, it does exist somewhere, but that particular one has
never been located. That's what I was trying to do with Ricky
and his two mates. We searched a couple of possible locations.
Ricky was interested in the story, and I thought: why not put
their archaeological training to the test. Leona would have told
you it quickly turned out to be a lost cause. Even if we had
found the site, it's not like it's something that would cause
Ricky to disappear. We're talking about stuff that happened
over one hundred and seventy-five years ago.'

Lenny spread his hands in a "what gives" gesture.

'Leona also told me about another massacre site Ricky
learnt about. A purportedly un-documented site. Do you know
about that?'

Lenny sat back in his chair and looked at Rory warily. He
began drumming his fingers on the table. Rory waited.

'He must have found Cec,' Lenny finally said.

'Cec?' Rory said.

'Cecil Gaynor. He's an old bloke who owns a farming
property near the Black Range.'

'That's west of the Grampians, right?'

'Geologically, it's part of the Grampians, but there's farmland in between.'

Lenny left it at that, still being hesitant.

'And …' Rory prompted.

'Cec's father, who settled the Black Range property way-back-when had married a Gunditj woman. She was from the Western District — red gum country where Cec's father grew up. His ancestors were pioneer squatters in that area of the Western District. The homestead is still there but no longer in the Gaynor family. It was sold in the 1980s.

'Anyway, Cec sought me out because he wanted to find out stuff about his Aboriginal roots and Aboriginal history in the area. He was pretty much raised white. I don't think he'd met an Aboriginal person after his mother died. He was still a teenager. Cec was well into his seventies when we met. He'd caught that bug about wanting to know where he came from. More in terms of local history, as it turned out because he'd already traced much of his family tree by then — black and white. From an Indigenous ignorant existence, he made a late-in-life connection with what had gone down in the early days.'

Lenny stalled again, thinking about how to take the story forward.

'Is that where the other massacre comes in?' Rory said.

'It is. When I told him about one of the Victoria Range massacres, something I mentioned caused his eyes to light up. He said it made sense of something he had read when he researched his family history — something Cec's great-great-grandfather wrote about to his family back in England. There was a whole batch of his ancestor's letters telling them about his pioneering life in Australia. Cec had made contact with descendants of those English relatives via Ancestry.com, one of which was in possession of the letters. They were happy for Cec to have the letters, and apparently, one letter referred disapprovingly to locals taking the law into their own hands on a neighbouring squatter's run. We're talking a massacre carried out by neighbours of Cec's white, great-great grandfather.'

Lenny sat back for the arrival of their bush foods platter. He ignored the intriguing array of tasting dishes to finish the story.

'Cec grew up in that area and sometimes visited his white uncles and aunties and cousins before the property was sold. He knew the area, and he reckoned there was enough detail in the letter for him to pinpoint where the atrocity took place and where the bodies might be buried.

'All of this added up, of course. In that first wave of European settlement of Victoria, killings and massacres were widespread. Also common was an unwillingness by Europeans to go on record about who was involved. Some were offended by their fellow Europeans' actions, but they too were reticent to reveal what they knew. Even back then, white fellas were in denial about invasion. Anyway, eat up.'

Lenny had a sardonic way of emphasising his point. Then he pointed to a small bowl of white meat.

'This one's crocodile. Give it a go, and don't tell me it tastes like chicken.'

'I thought it might be emu,' Rory said before he began chewing the crocodile.

'Nah. The emu meat is pretty much red. What'd ya think of the croc?'

Rory chewed a bit more and pulled an unconvinced expression.

'Not much taste at all. I'll try some of this with it,' he said, reaching for native chutney. He broke the small wattle seed damper to accompany it.

Lenny watched on. Rory was feeling the pressure for his taste buds to be blown away. He began nodding appreciatively as he chewed. 'Mmm,' he offered without faking it.

Lenny joined in the repast — satisfied that the meal was amply appreciated. As dining settled into a more leisurely pace, Rory got matters back on script.

'So how come you never located Cecil's purported massacre site?'

'Well, Cec was coy about showing me the letters. I went along with him all the same — in the name of history, like. So, one day, he and I drove over to the property where he calculated the massacre took place.

'Like I said, the property in question and Cec's forebears' farm had originally been neighbouring squatters' runs. And as you probably know, squatters were the first Europeans to move onto the black fellas' land. They were the ones who gained exclusive use of vast tracts of Victoria and they brooked no intruders, notwithstanding they were the only intruders in sight. By the time their empires were carved up in the 1860s for ownership by the broader public, the invasion war with the Aboriginal inhabitants had been fought — mostly violently — and won. After that, the squatters went on to win the war on land ownership too. When their runs were eventually subdivided for selection by the general public, cashed up squatters were able to retain much of their original holding, usually by foul means, like installing family members as dummy owners and cherry-picking access to all the water sources. If all else failed, they weren't averse to bribing the land office officials.

'And that's what happened with the property we're talking about. Most of the original run remained in the family after being subdivided for selection. Its area only increased during economic slumps as they acquired smaller neighbours going under. What's more, the empire, which is still pretty substantial, was held by the same family living in the same grand homestead. When Cec and I rocked up and knocked on that door, the last thing they wanted to hear, especially from two Aboriginal blokes standing on their front step, was that their family were responsible for carrying out a massacre and the bodies were buried there. "Do you mind if we dig the place up and prove it?" We got short shrift quicker than a didgeri can doo … as well as threats of bankrupt-producing legal actions landing in our mailboxes.'

The story left Rory curious. Lenny was obviously not the type to roll over.

'The policeman in me says: how come that was the end of that if you had documented evidence? Surely you could have taken the matter further by some other means or channels.'

'That's right. The fact that the property was still in the hands of the original family, and they were denying it, that made it an authentic battle. This was a chance for us descendants of the country's traditional owners to go back into battle with the original perpetrators. That got the adrenalin going. As far as I was concerned, Cec and my encounter with them had only been round one.'

'And yet I'm not sensing a happy ending.'

'Within twenty-four hours, Cec's house burnt down. The letters went with it.'

'Suspicious?'

'Well, they knew exactly who Cec was when he told them his surname. But it didn't matter. We didn't have the letters. I mean, we are big on oral history; that's the foundation of Aboriginal history. It's how our knowledge has been retained over millennia. But this wasn't oral history. This was a written European account of something that happened, white man's proof, and now it was destroyed. It was not knowledge that had been passed down to Cec by his father and his father before him. It was simply something Cec had read in recent times. The only living person who had seen it was Cec. His English relatives may have also read it in passing, but not with particular memory or appreciation for local detail that Cec had. I trusted Cec, but we had nothing that would prove to anyone that there might be something in what he was saying. You're a copper. You know what I'm talking about. We had to let it go.'

'Did Cecil let it go?'

'If he did, it would have been begrudgingly, but ... to be honest, I don't know what he would have done if he had his way. But it wasn't his call.'

The coffees arrived, and both men paused to partake, both content to reflect on Lenny's unsated tale.

'Did Ricky ever meet Cecil?' Rory finally interrupted their reveries.

'Not with me. I told Ricky the story, and I remember how it fired him up. He asked a lot of questions. He'd become more interested in that invasion period than the older archaeological stuff. But as far as I was concerned, it was a story with a start and a middle, and now it had an end. A heartbreaking end, but we're Aboriginal. Our history's full of heartbreaking encounters with whites.'

'From what Leona told me, Ricky did meet Cecil. She didn't know him by name. She only mentioned him as a local farmer who told Ricky about an unrecorded killing site.'

'Well, I suppose it wouldn't have been too hard for Ricky to track down Cec, but if he did, he never told me. It's too late to find out in any case. Cec died a few years ago. Probably not that long after Ricky went missing.'

Rory stared at the mountain until his next thought came.

'Assuming he did meet Cecil ... and he heard the story directly from Cecil. Do you reckon he could have fired Ricky up enough to follow through in any way ... perhaps on his own?'

The path of Lenny's coffee cup towards his lips froze an inch short of its destination.

'Fuck. Is that where all this is headed. You think Ricky could have stuck his nose in where it wasn't welcome? Is that the reason he ended up missing?'

'You've met Ricky. You've met the property owner. You tell me.'

'I can tell you it wouldn't have been pretty if the two of them ever met. But …'

'Can you tell me about this property? Do you remember where it was, who owns it?'

'I remember what the property is called if you can believe it. They named it Kilmany, after a place in Scotland. And I can also tell you the name of the owner. You don't forget a piece of work like that either. His name was Elliot Claymore.'

Tahlia was already waiting for him at Halls Gap's Harvest café — a pattern was emerging. Rory was up for his fourth coffee for the day. Tahlia stuck to water.

'What'd ya think of Brambuk?' she greeted him.

'Yeah, I liked it. Impressive.'

'And Lenny?'

'Same. Knows his stuff … even if he doesn't mind using it for effect.'

'He's a popular guide and a passionate advocate. With Lenny, you're always going to get it full-on with a healthy dose of black-fella humour.'

'Fair enough. I was surprised — even though I wasn't surprised — that Lenny wasn't interviewed by my colleagues when Ricky went missing. He'd spent plenty of one-on-one time with Ricky, delving into that early European settlement era. Lenny enlightened him about massacres known to have taken place … as well as a previously unheard-of one that

Lenny had recently become aware of. A local farmer named Cecil Gaynor had discovered reference to it in his ancestor's correspondence. Ricky may have contacted him.'

'This is all news to me … that Ricky was interested in that stuff. That there were massacres around here. I mean …'

'From what Lenny told me, there were a few massacres in and around the Grampians. The newly discovered one was further west. More Western District country, where Cecil's ancestors were from. Cecil ended up becoming a farmer near the Black Range. He had Aboriginal blood, but he passed away a few years ago. I'll be following it up with any family he may have, but I'm worried I might be too late. Now that he's passed on.'

Tahlia slumped in her chair and sighed.

'It's slow work. Be patient. Have you found a number for Ethan Hall yet? The survivor in the car crash?'

'No,' Tahlia answered despondently.

'Well, keep trying. This is how it works. Slow gathering of little bits of knowledge.'

'Yeah, okay.'

'You don't sound it,' Rory observed.

'Like, it's just all this stuff that happened, and I'm only learning about it now — four years after the event. Like … Lenny knew about this stuff, and he knew who I was when I moved here. Why didn't he say something?'

'It's not Lenny's fault. How would he know there could be a connection with any of the stuff he deals with all the time and Ricky going missing? Just as likely there's not. There's nothing to say any of it is connected. It's just part of the picture of what Ricky was up to before he went missing. Doesn't archaeology work something like that too?'

'Totally, when you put it like that. It's hard not to be impatient just the same.'

'Well, think of it as an archaeology investigation … and Ethan Hall … let me know if you can't find a number for him, and I'll get my colleagues on the case.'

'No. He'll be around. Leave it with me.'

Chapter 19

Travis Vella stood by the entrance to Police headquarters. Rory did a double-take as he fumbled for his electronic entry pass.

'What're you doing here?'

'The company I work for has a Melbourne office. I made sure I had business to do down here.'

'You want to talk?'

'Yeah. But only to you … and not in there. Off the record.'

Rory looked at him, wondering how to play it. It was clear that it was going to be Travis Vella's way or no way.

'Do you want to go for a coffee then?'

'Yeah. You know somewhere where Cockburn won't show up?'

Rory gave a wry grin.

'I know a place. It's a bit of a walk. Let's go.'

They stepped over to the corner, and Rory pressed the traffic light button.

'You been waiting long?' he asked as they waited.

'Nearly two hours. I was about to give the idea away.'

'You're lucky someone didn't come out and arrest you — loitering around police headquarters. You're probably a CCTV star and don't know it.'

Travis looked worried.

'Don't worry. I'll calm 'em down if anyone asks me about it.'

They arrived at a city-fringe café nestled in the shop frontage of a high rise. They managed to score one of the half-tables with two chairs along the sidewall. Most commuters were opting for takeaways to carry into the office. They both ordered double shot blacks which they were forced to hunch over in the cramped row of mini tables. It was going to be an intimate conversation — whether they wanted it to be or not.

'Cockburn won't show up here; they serve vegan. The coffee's good too.'

Mention of Cockburn set Travis Vella off.

'You were with him on the interview. You know he's got me in the gun, big-time.'

'What makes you think I have a different view?'

'You can think that if you like. I understand it's your job to consider all scenarios. That's what I'm counting on you doing. You're my only hope in all this.'

Rory fondled the sachet of sugar that came with his coffee. He had no use for it other than allowing himself time to think before he responded.

'I know you said you want to talk to me off the record, which you're doing right now … and I'm listening off the record. But you have to appreciate that I can't talk off the record, and I can't un-hear stuff. What I will say though, is: I'll certainly be looking at every possibility … as I always do. Unfortunately for you, that's only going to take things so far in this case. There just aren't that many conceivable possibilities. You're going to have to do better than tell me you didn't do it and rely on my better nature.'

'I'm not here to rely on your better nature. I've been wracking my brain about other possibilities. Trying to fathom why someone would want to kill Gloria in the first place and why her body ended up where it did. It's …' He flayed his hands searching for a word. '… absolutely baffling. For argument's sake, if you ruled me out as a suspect, who do you reckon did it and why?'

Rory wasn't ready for the question. His blank expression showed it.

'See. You're not considering any other possibility.'

Rory played a straight bat.

'We'll see where the investigation takes us. In the meantime, what have you come up with? Isn't that why I'm here?'

This time Travis Vella took time thinking about what he would say.

'In my job, I often get caught up in battles between miners and farmers. In theory, the community consultation and PR have been completed by the mining company before I drive through someone's gate and begin the exploration work I do, which is usually non-invasive stuff. Low impact. Like geophysical surveys, seismic surveys, other GPRs … sorry … ground-penetrating radar, drone-borne stuff — things like that. Not even drilling. That comes later.'

Rory cut through Travis Vella's plethora of jargon.

'You make enemies.'

'Sometimes I encounter upset people. Usually, I can deal with that. I've been at it a long time.'

'But you made an enemy.'

'Only a couple in my career, and only once when I was working in the Grampians area.'

'And who was this person?'

'A landholder called Elliot Claymore.'

Whoa!

Rory's mind raced. Surely there was only one Elliot Claymore in the world. And here he was, cracking a mention for a second time in as many days … in totally unrelated cases. *What am I dealing with here*? According to Lenny Dalton, he was a totally un-endearing character whose name cropped up, albeit obliquely at this stage, in relation to Ricky Lock's disappearance. Nothing certain there. Now Travis Vella was fingering the same person as an alternative suspect for Gloria Vella's murder. The cases were worlds apart, but suddenly they weren't. Who was Elliot Claymore?

Travis could see he'd struck a nerve.

'What? Do you know him?'

Rory recovered enough to fudge.

'I've never met anyone with that name. You better tell me about him.'

'I only want *you* looking into this. Not Cockburn. That's the deal.'

'You've already given me this bloke's name. And it's Cockburn's case. At some stage, he has to know.'

'I know you can't un-hear it, but I'm relying on your integrity.'

Rory began stroking his chin. Bringing Cockburn into the picture at this stage would mean Cockburn trampling all over the Ricky Lock investigation, let alone more damaging encounters between Cockburn and Tahlia. Although the question answered itself, that's not how he sold it to Travis Vella.

'Don't confuse whose side I'm on here. As far as integrity goes, the police conduct unit would have it that I take this to Cockburn right now. But okay. I'll follow it up myself …' Rory said. Then qualified, '… at this stage. So, tell me about Elliot Claymore.'

Travis Vella recognised he'd taken it as far as he could. He sighed, then pushed on.

'Elliot Claymore is the last man standing in one of those squatting dynasties. What I mean by that is, he's old, he doesn't have an heir, and he's struggling to keep on top of things. Not so much physically, because the old prick is still as fit as, but business-wise he's being left for dead. I mean, back then, he didn't have a mobile or Wi-Fi. For all I know, he probably still hasn't.'

He gave a shake of the head that said, *hopeless.*

'These days, most of those mammoth farming empires that have been around since European settlement are run by managers working for foreign or corporate interests. There are still properties where the sons or daughters have hung around and made a fist of it, but the stratospheric sheep graziers' lifestyle that existed when the Western District was one of the wealthiest areas on Earth no longer exists — except in Elliot Claymore's mind. He's got the manor to prove it … and the manner. Of course, that doesn't endear him to anyone, at least not anyone I spoke to. You still hear about shearers giving the place a wide berth. The tucker on offer was always shit, a boiled egg if you were lucky, they'd tell you, and no knocking-off if the sheep were wet.'

Travis Vella made a point of looking hard at Rory to drive home his next point.

'If you go there, you'll see what I mean — all faded glory. Just the look of the place. He still gets about in his 1970s Jaguar limo, spewing more black smoke from the exhaust than a steam engine. The word in the pub was, his wife of forty-odd years had not long walked out on him. That was set to cost him a bob … or at least a good many acres. Maybe that's why he's as bitter as all fuck.

'I met his wife once. Carol knows her. I bumped into the two of them in town one day. Me and Carol had started seeing each other, but not publicly. We played it cool, but not so cool we didn't stop for a hello chat. Anyway, Carol introduced us. Eva, a looker who'd worn rather well, I have to say, pricked up her ears when Carol referred to me as a Sydneysider. It turns out Eva grew up there and only moved to Victoria when she and Claymore got married.'

'She's from Sydney? How did Claymore crack onto someone from Sydney?' Rory asked.

'Apparently, as a young man, he was on the board of a national woolgrowers' agency and attended meetings up there. Eva worked at the agency. He clearly punched above his weight, so he must have had something going for him — apart from shitloads of money — but I couldn't see it. I've never met anyone like him. The first time I met him was when I went there to sound him out about surveying his place for minerals. While I was running through my usual spiel, I had the growing feeling that he just wanted to put his big hands around my throat and throttle me. He was seething so much my voice started to shake. He's a big, ugly hooer who'd have no trouble doing it.'

'And ...' Rory said.

'He heard me out, albeit with chilling unwillingness oozing out of him. I think he let me babble on to make sure his scariness was having an impact. Anything I said was simply not registering, be it the prospect of money for him or local community good. It all went in one ear and out the other. Then he declined consent for us to enter onto his land ... ever. I was on my own, and I was outta there so fucking fast.'

'So, he killed your wife for that?'

'I'm getting there. A couple of days later, I sent Tony to another job on the same list of properties. A job where the owner *had* provided consent. The only problem was, we managed to fuck up which property Tony was meant to go to. He ended up in one of Claymore's paddocks and managed to complete a fair whack of underground geology imaging before

Claymore showed up. He virtually frog-marched Tony off the place, but not before he demanded whatever "contraption" the data was stored on. Of course, it was on a hard drive embedded in the instrument, and Tony couldn't extract it for him on the spot. Claymore put an axe through it. Tony reckons he only got out alive because Claymore knew that people knew he was there. He actually asked Tony: "Does anyone know you're here?" He told Claymore I knew. That I sent him.'

'Did you go to the Police?'

'No. I didn't think Claymore would be making the incident known to anyone, so we wrote it off. If we took it to the cops and it ended up in court, it'd be a PR disaster for us. Our reputation would take a hit, whatever the outcome. That's why I went back there to apologise for surveying his property without his consent. Risk mitigation, I thought. Risk un-mitigation in hindsight.'

'How bad did it go, then?' Rory asked.

'When I finally found him, he accused me of doing it deliberately and that I'd pay. He said I would suffer like he did. If I'd thought he'd sounded chilling at our first meeting, then this was off the scale. This time he was calm, and icy, and totally terrifying.'

'And how long was this before Gloria went missing?'

'Only a week, ten days. Something like that.'

'And you think he would do that. Seek out your wife. He'd know you were married if you wore a ring, but he'd have no idea you lived in Sydney. And why your wife? Why not you? Straight off the bat, there's a whole truckload of "ifs" in this story.'

'I know all that, but one thing struck me since I've tried to make sense of this. He said he would make me "suffer like him". At that stage, he'd hadn't got over his wife walking out on him. His bitterness was probably ramped out of control as settlement of divorce finances kicked in. You're a cop. You know what those things can drive men to do, let alone a nut job like Claymore. Wait till you meet him.'

Travis Vella hadn't finished his coffee. It was cold. Rory looked at it and pondered.

'Okay, I'll have a look at it. Email some details to this address.' He gave him a card. 'The diary of your meetings with Claymore. Tony's full name and number. Where he's working now.' Rory thought he'd finished, then added, 'Are there any other enemies you're aware of?'

'None like Claymore. None who would actually do the job.'

'Okay. I'd better get back to the office. I'll be in touch … or Cockburn might. I'll only be able to take it so far without bringing him in. But I can still look over his shoulder if that's any comfort.'

'Yeah, well, do what you can.'

'And does Lincoln Renfrey know you were coming to see me,' Rory said, referring to Travis's lawyer.

'No. He's supposed to be an old school friend, but he'd probably charge me for the privilege of phoning him to let him know I came to see you.'

'Shit,' Travis Vella said as they rounded the corner on the walk back. 'That's my Hilux parked across the road. Looks like I got a ticket.'

Rory crossed the road with Travis Vella to the twin-cab workhorse fitted with overhead racks and large, locked tradie-equipment boxes. There was no company logo displayed on the vehicle.

'You fly incognito. Is that a mining company thing?'

'It's pretty much mandatory in Victoria, where most of our interest lies below farming land. Nearly everything north and west of the Grampians has mineral sands full of titanium, zircon, even gold. It doesn't always pay to draw attention.'

Rory peered through the vehicle's side window. Among some mail on the back seat were several subscription copies of GeoScienceWorld journal, still in their clear plastic mailing covers.

'The mining journal gives you away, though', Rory observed.

'I 'spose so. I always chuck them in when I'm on the road, thinking I'll have the time to read them. It never happens.'

Natalie had the crime board in order. The collection of photos among felt-tipped pen labels and a spaghetti of arrows told a complicated but damning tale for Travis Vella. She was adding some final touches when Rory arrived.

'You want to get a coffee before we start?' Bourke asked Rory.

'I'm right. I just had one.'

Bourke turned back to the crime board and nodded sagely. Natalie looked on smugly. She was in full presentation mode. Not only had she crafted the crime board, but she had also returned from her trip to Balmoral and was ready for show and tell. Her dark hair was not in its usual "up" do. She also wore a cropped red jacket over her not-loose fitting black top and trousers.

'Okay then. Tell us what you found out in Balmoral, Natalie?' Bourke said.

'Everything and nothing. Everybody remembers Travis Vella. He spent enough time there for people to know who he was, and everybody liked Travis. People could quote entire conversations they had with him. Trouble was, no one could remember actual dates. I asked far and wide and got nothing that added to his alibi from Carol Warren. I don't know why he thought he needed to be coy about seeing Carol either, because everybody knew he was rooting her, to use their word. 'tis a country village after all. One other thing: I don't know why he chose the caravan park ahead of the pub. I tell you, I was back in County Cork heaven. I mean, my bedroom was basic, but Beryl, the cook, would always make sure there were meals there for me, even when she'd gone home for the day. A bar full of friendly souls just down the hall; one young fella pulled out a guitar, and we sang. No kids or husband to bother me. It was like bein' at me mam's again. Travis Vella didn't know what was good for him.'

'Remind me not to send you further south to Killarney, Natalie. We might never see you again. Did you find out about the fossickers' holes being filled in?'

'Again, everything and nothing. I found out who filled the actual hole. Parks Victoria did a few abandoned ones not that long ago. They had complaints about one particular one being dangerous. Before that, Hal Rogers filled a really deep hole for the old-timer from the Wimmera. Nobody seems to know his name, and Hal hasn't seen him since. He reckons he's probably dead or in a nursing home by now. Hal said he filled that hole around the time Gloria Travis' body was dumped there. He's been to the site since it hit the media and he's pretty sure he filled the hole she was dumped in … the hole next to Terry's hole. He said he doesn't remember seeing a blue tarp in it before he started. Someone obviously shovelled some soil over it by hand. So, there's your answer … but so what?'

'It's all part of the puzzle, Natalie. Good work. What about you, Gary?'

'I was right about Carol Warren being a scheming gold digger. She took her in-laws to the cleaners.'

'She didn't get divorced Gary. Her husband died of cancer. You don't plan that.' Natalie interrupted.

'Same difference. She'd been on the scene for five minutes, and she ended up walking away with hundreds of thousands. Her husband died without making a will and her in-laws challenged what was due to her as next of kin. The court settlement of her husband's estate ate deep into what her father-in-law and brother-in-law regarded as "family" assets. Fool them for letting the family farm structure evolve the way it had. It helped that she had pretty handy legal reps while they allowed themselves to be saddled with a duty barrister.

Amateurs up against a real pro. They're still paying her off. She's probably getting half of every year's wool clip.'

'So, she's savvy,' Natalie defended.

'Ruthless, conniving, devious, conspiring, merciless.'

Rory also had his say.

'Come on, Gary. Even if all of those adjectives were true and you accused her of as much in court, it doesn't make her a perjurer when it comes to Vella's alibi.'

Bourke came to Cockburn's defence.

'I know what you're saying Rory, but this is such a compelling set of circumstances and even though Natalie thinks she found out nothing, that nothing is: nobody else being able to say Travis Vella was where he said he was when his wife went missing. Let's just put that in our back pocket for now. You got any other ideas?'

'One. I just had coffee with Travis Vella,' Rory revealed.

'What? Here in Melbourne?' Cockburn said.

Rory raised his eyes at Cockburn as if peering over a pair of glasses.

'What's his story?' Bourke asked.

'He's shitting himself. He's realised how undeniable it all seems and how clearly Gary has him in his sights. He doesn't want anything to do with you. He insisted I didn't tell you.' Rory said, turning to Cockburn.

'Mutual. Does he want to do some kind of deal?'

'Nothing like that. He gave me the name of someone he reckons could have it in for him. It's a landholder down that way who he got into a serious blue with about exploring on his land.'

'Is he serious? He has a blue in Victoria, and that person heads off to Sydney, kills his wife and transports her body back to Victoria for no one to ever find? Sounds like a pretty desperate story to concoct, Rory.' Bourke said.

'Yeah, I know. And it raises a lot of even harder questions, but ....'

'Oh, for fuck's sake,' Cockburn said. 'This is beyond desperate. You're not going to give it oxygen, are you? We should be spending time building the real case. There's CCTV footage that the New South cops collected. We need to go through all that; mobile phone records to dig up and review; public appeals; trace the tarp. Forensics didn't find prints on the tarp, but they're still testing for other stuff. We haven't scratched the surface. We'll nail this prick. And even if we don't end up with a silver bullet, the last thing we'll need is the waters being muddied.'

'Sounds like you've got a feeling about this fella, Rory?' Natalie offered on a calmer note.

'It's not as far-fetched as it sounds on face value. I'm going to be down that way on the Ricky Lock case. I want to at least meet this guy. See if he's the piece of work Travis Vella says he is.'

Bourke had the final word.

'By all means, have a look at it, Rory, but don't make it a mission in life.'

Chapter 20

'*I tracked down Ethan Hall,*' Rory heard Tahlia tell him over the phone. He walked out onto the tiny balcony of Michelle's apartment.

'Well done. Where is he? Can you send me his details?'

'*I can. But that's not how this is gonna work. He doesn't want to speak to you unless I'm there. He's been fucked over by cops too many times.*'

Rory drew breath through his nose. It was a stark reminder that the Force's prominent acknowledgement of traditional custodians of the land and a swag of Aboriginal liaison officers didn't heal all wounds.

'The sins of my colleagues.'

'*If you like.*'

'I don't like. Anyway, where does he live? Where is he happy to meet?'

'*He still lives in Warrnambool, but I've talked him into meeting us where they found the car. I want to see it for myself. That suits him. He's working up that way with a blue gum plantation harvesting crew.*'

'I thought he said the dead driver found Ricky's car and that he wasn't there.'

'*He did say that to the cops. He wasn't stupid enough to let them pin a car theft on him.*'

'Fair enough. So where do we meet him?'

'*You're not going to believe this.*'

'Did you ever have that feeling that things are slotting together a bit too well in a case? You know, too many coincidences to be a coincidence?'

'No. But wouldn't that be a good thing?' Michelle said.

'I dunno yet.'

Rory was still standing in her balcony doorway with his phone in his hand. Michelle was at the kitchen bench in her house-wear — cuffed black tracky dacks and a sleeveless grey tee shirt. It couldn't hide her long curvy figure. Rory's mind drifted.

'The nachos are in the oven. Just doing some guacamole. I hope you don't mind things hot. I make it with a bite.'

Rory re-surfaced. 'I'll be able to douse it with my Corona. I brought the perfect beer without knowing it.'

He grabbed his beer from the bench and raised it to clink a toast with Michelle's Corona.

'To our night in.'

'To a night in. Now tell me about these coincidences.'

She joined him on the couch, slung both legs across his lap and took another sip of Corona.

Rory's offhand toast was an acknowledgement of the capricious state of domestic bliss that had settled on their evening. Michelle knew it too but thought that saying it out loud might break the spell. She had sought to move matters on. He was oblivious to the hint.

'Suddenly talking work seems wrong. This is too … tranquil,' he said, wallowing in the pleasure of everyday normality that had struck him out of the blue.

'You're too easily pleased. It's just nachos and a beer. There might be some ice cream left in the tub.'

Finally, she succeeded in moving Rory away from tempting fate.

'I had a different dessert in mind,' he responded.

'Easy tiger. We'll get there. We haven't eaten yet, and I want to hear about your case. I miss problem-solving like this. I might even be able to help. Don't forget my super-power was reading people. And if you're worried about it affecting me, I think I'm detached enough not to buy into any of it. Trust me.'

He looked hard at her, trying to figure out if it was a road he'd go down if their situations were switched.

'Stop worrying about it. It's not a no-no in the PTSD sufferers' rulebook. Just tell me. I was married to a cop. This is how it works best.'

'You know as well as I do that there's no such rulebook.'

'Exactly. So, you won't be breaking any rules.'

Rory caved.

'Well, you know this body we found in the gemstone mine, it turned out to be the missing wife of a mining geologist from Sydney named Travis Vella. He was doing company exploration work near the Grampians when she went missing four and a half years ago. That seemed like a flawless alibi for someone who'd gone missing in Sydney … until the New South Wales cops found a hole in his claimed whereabouts that gave him enough time to drive there and back.'

'What? A major trip like that and no electronic records? Mobile phone data, credit card use, or CCTV he could rely on?' she asked.

'None of that. But when the New South cops backed him into that corner, he came clean, admitting he was having an affair that his wife had recently learnt about — with a woman in Victoria. His new woman ended up vouching for him. They had been keeping their relationship quiet because she was not long widowed, and it could have influenced a legal battle she was in over her husband's estate. They're still together and now and they've got two kids. As well as enduring the cops' suspicions at that time, he copped the News South Wales media intimating he was responsible for her disappearance.'

'So, all that's back under the microscope because her body showed up, smack-bang in the middle of his interstate alibi?' Michelle concluded.

'Exactly. And as bulletproof, as his alibi might sound, I think he was doubting it himself after his wife's body turned up where it did … and Cockburn interviewed him. After that experience, he put his own mind to what might have happened and came to me on the quiet — sans Cockburn. He told me about a run-in he'd had with a psycho farmer he approached about surveying land under the mineral exploration licence he was working. The farmer is a lord-of-the-manor type on his family's original squatters run. Anyway, psycho-farmer ended up putting an axe into his seismic measuring equipment and threatening Travis — he would make him suffer like he did. Travis thinks that could have been a reference to the farmer's wife having just left him after forty years. I haven't met this farmer or checked much of this out yet. His name is Elliot Claymore.'

'All very interesting, but where are the coincidences you mentioned?'

The oven-timer told them the nachos were ready. They decamped from the sofa to the table. Rory poured them both a red wine. The messy finger food task at hand left the story on hold for the duration. They were several napkins in and down to the sloppy last bits when Rory complimented the chef.

'You nailed that guacamole.'

'Yeah, yeah. Are you nearly done? I'm ready to hear part two.'

'Okay. I'll get us a top-up first.'

With drinks in hand, the story resumed back on the couch.

'Tahlia, the cultural heritage officer you saw me with at Dunkeld is a qualified archaeologist. She lives at Halls Gap. Apparently, her brother, who is also an archaeologist, went missing from Halls Gap a few years ago. She brought up the fact that the case was way under-investigated and pretty much dismissed as an Aboriginal kid gone walkabout … and he's still missing.'

'So, Saint Rory suddenly has two cases,' Michelle said.

Rory pouted but pressed on.

'After speaking to a couple of the last people to see him, I found out he's on the trail of an unrecorded Aboriginal massacre that took part in colonial times. Purportedly, it was a hushed-up massacre carried out by settlers on their original squatter's run.'

Michelle lit up. 'And that's your coincidence. It was Elliot Claymore's property.'

'That's only the first coincidence. The place is called "Kilmany", believe it or not, and it looks as though Tahlia's brother could have headed there sometime before he went missing. Two Indigenous blokes, Lenny and Cecil, who told Tahlia's brother about the alleged massacre, had already been to Kilmany and got short shrift, as well as formally threatened legal action for their trouble. A possible trail was starting to emerge.

'Then Tahlia phoned — the call I had earlier tonight. Six months after her brother went missing, his missing car was in an accident and written off. The young blokes driving it — one of them was also Aboriginal — said they found it in some bush. No cops followed that up … or believed them, I take it. Tahlia wasn't satisfied. She managed to chase down one of the occupants herself. She spoke to him today, and he's agreed to take us to where the car was found. Guess where?'

'Not at Claymore's property. That would be too cute for words.'

'No. Not there. Apparently, they found it not far from the gemstone site.'

'Ooooooh.'

'Ooooooh indeed. Do you want to think about that?'

'No. I've kept up. What do you want to know?'

'Tell me,' he said. 'When I find myself on a case in the middle of nowhere, how can another case land on my doorstep, totally unrelated in any way, and those two cases start overlapping like this? What's going on?'

'Well, to begin with. They are connected.'

'How so.'

'I don't know, but you'll find out. And I don't think Travis Vella did it. I say that based on some of the little things. Like the fact that he came to you. I don't think that would happen if he was guilty.'

'Anything else?'

'Yeah. There's more to Elliot Claymore than his wife leaving him. I'm not sure what, but his behaviour with Ricky's mates, Lenny and Cecil, and then with Travis Vella, doesn't sit right. I think you need to do more digging there.'

'That's it?'

'Yeah. Why? Do you see things differently?'

'No. They're things I've been thinking but haven't said out loud.'

He looked at her … and looked.

'I think it might be time for you to show your appreciation for my criminal consultancy services.'

Chapter 21

The tic-tic-tic sound of the unmarked police car's engine cooling down seemed amplified in the empty forest. It had just been parked at a fork in the dirt track, two kilometres short of arriving at the gemstone site. Tahlia and Rory alighted to stretch their legs after the drive from Halls Gap.

'He's late. That's always a good sign … not. D'ya reckon he's gonna show?'

Tahlia shrugged. She had left her Parks Victoria outfit at home. Rory wondered if it was deliberate. Maybe the authority-reluctant Ethan was averse to any uniform. He didn't ask.

'And you're sure this is where he wanted to meet?'

'Give it ten. Then I'll try his mobile. If he's not here in twenty, we give it a miss and head to this other place you want to go to.'

Rory had obtained the address of Elliot Claymore — an hour or so's drive from where they were meeting Ethan Hall. It was too near not to kill two birds with one stone. He would pay Claymore a surprise visit to ask him about his encounters with Travis Vella. He had no intention of perusing anything to do with Ricky Lock on this visit. So far, Rory had nothing concrete to link Claymore to Ricky. Nor did he intend to mention that possibility to Tahlia. The last thing he wanted to do was to create false hope.

Nonetheless, in his own head, he hadn't dismissed the possibility that Ricky may have crossed Claymore's path in his quest to identify the massacre site. In that regard, the fact that Tahlia was in tow was not without usefulness, albeit a long shot. If Claymore had in fact encountered Ricky, which surely wouldn't have gone well, then perhaps Tahlia's family resemblance might elicit a reaction when they met Claymore. All that could happen without Tahlia being any the wiser.

'I think I can hear a car now,' Tahlia said after five.

Ethan Hall arrived in a well-aged mustard coloured Subaru Brumby 4WD ute fitted with a roll bar and bull bar. In his mid-twenties, Aboriginal, unsmiling and dressed in work clobber — navy drill pants and a yellow hi-viz shirt that had already seen a few days' hard slog.

Hellos were perfunctory, small talk non-existent. Rory and Tahlia's "thank yous" were met with a shrug.

'You'll need to hop in the Brumby. You won't make it in that,' he nodded to the unmarked police car.

'Do you reckon it'll be okay here?' Rory asked Tahlia.

'If it isn't, I know where to find a cop.'

Ethen began shovelling stuff from the passenger seat of the Brumby into the ute tray. Clothes, a couple of power tools, a new pair of shoes in a box, and a fishing rod.

'I'll go in the back. It's not far, is it Ethan?' Tahlia said.

'What do you mean?' Rory asked.

'There's only one passenger seat. You have that. I'll stand in the back.'

'I don't mind,' Rory offered without enthusiasm.

'Nah. It's okay. You get the gates, though.'

They took the fork away from the gem site and were at a gate in no time. Tahlia and Ethan were patient as Rory figured out the wire-and-stick securing mechanism. The gate opened onto cleared hills that rolled down to a horizon-to-horizon expanse of dead trees in water — Rocklands Reservoir. The enticing Black Range rose on its opposite bank.

The fence line formed a hard divide between bushland and open paddock. Ethan drove across the extensive open paddock to a side fence. As they neared, it was clear the fence was an antique of the pre galvanised-wire era. Its rusty wires lay on the ground where random posts had rotted at the base or been eaten through by termites. He drove over a section of prostrate fence, back into the bush. There was little understorey, allowing him to weave between trees to the head of a gully. He came to a halt about a hundred metres down the other side of the rise, turned the engine off and turned to Rory.

'This is where we found it.'

They alighted.

'See? The car was behind that rise.'

He pointed.

'Like they didn't want anyone to see it from the paddock. The key was still in it.' Ethan explained. 'It was covered in dust and leaves 'n' shit. Like it had been abandoned for months.'

'Anything in it?'

'Nah. Nothing special anyway — not like a wallet or phone.'

Rory was surprised at how quickly they'd reached the place.

'How far do you reckon we are from the gemstone site?' he asked, turning to Tahlia.

'Two kilometres as the crow flies. No more,' she said distractedly. She had honed in on a completely faded and mouldy cloth seat cover. There was grass growing on a corner of it where dust and mulch had encroached over the years.

'That was wet from rain. The driver's window was down a bit. We chucked it,' Ethan said.

Tahlia lifted a corner of the stiffened seat cover. It unfolded to expose sections that had escaped fading from the sun's rays. The original colour and pattern were unmarred.

'It's Ricky's,' she said and dropped it to clasp her mouth. 'I remember it from when he drove home to Murwillumbah.'

'Leave it until I photograph it,' Rory said.

Tahlia stood, soaked in shock and sorrow, looking at the scene. After a while, she backed away to sit on the grass. A tear rolled from each eye to her mouth, closed tightly in heavy silence. Rory walked the scene looking for any other debris or clues not consumed by nature. There were none. He took more photographs and lifted the seat cover into the ute tray using a stick. Ethan lit a cigarette and waited.

That done, Rory came behind Ethan, placed a hand on his shoulder and said, 'Thanks, mate.'

'No worries.'

He squatted beside Tahlia.

'You want more time?'

She brushed the tears.

'Nah. He wasn't here. It was just his car. Let's get out of here.'

'Okay. You have the seat this time.'

'It's still here,' Rory said when they arrived back at the unmarked police car parked in the bush.

'More chance of it being struck by a meteorite than being stolen out here,' Ethan said. He had left the Subaru Brumby running while Rory and Tahlia hopped out, then spoke to them with his arm resting on the open driver's side window. He wasn't hanging around.

'Good to know,' Rory found himself saying inanely. 'Anyway. Thanks for showing us where the car was found. It's important. It could help us find out what happened to Ricky.'

'Yeah, bro,' Tahlia added and gave a fist bump.

'No worries, See ya's,' and he was on his way back to re-join the harvesting crew in neighbourhood blue gum plantations. In an Australian environmental role reversal of sorts, prime farming land, swallowed up for forestry investments in the 2000s, was in the process of being returned to the state of being parkland, "sprinkled with only a few trees", that greeted the first Europeans.

There was much silence in the next leg of their journey. Tahlia remained in her own world, looking blankly out the car's side window. Speech only broke out to decide which direction to take at each corner. They wove roughly west along single-car widths of bitumen, slowing radically to navigate the grassy verge around the occasional oncoming vehicle or tractor. An accompanying bush wave was mandatory — a finger lifted laconically from the hand gripping the top of the steering wheel.

The further west they went, the more the "red-gum country" became the quintessential Australian grazing idyll. The mammoth gums became statelier, the rolling hills grander, in natural parkland Major Mitchell laid the first pair of European eyes upon. It stirred a rhapsodizing account from the Scotsman.

The whole country consisted of open forest land, on which grew a few gum-trees (or eucalypti) with banksia, and, occasionally, a few casuarina ... I was struck with the beauty and substantial value of the country ... it seemed that the land was everywhere good, alike beautiful; all parts were verdant, whether on the finely varied hills or the equally romantic vales, which seemed to open in endless succession on both banks of the river ...

The tableau spread out before Rory and Tahlia as they crossed an un treed dome of the Dundas tablelands. The scene lost none of its appeal from the addition of fences and a few roads. Rory added to Mitchell's elucidation.

'Not fucking bad, hey?'

'Still part of Jardwadjali country. They fought hard in the frontier wars,' Tahlia answered — seemingly unmoved by the splendour.

More like her brother than she knows, Rory noted to himself.

Soon they were passing through a driveway entrance flanked by stone walls upon which "Kilmany" was carved in large letters. A missing finial on one of the piers heralded the encroaching decay Travis Vella spoke of.

'Kilmany?' Tahlia queried, incredulously, despite being unaware they may be visiting the scene of a massacre.

Rory took his time along the cypress-lined avenue. The driveway curved in an arc around the head of a broad valley to a commanding rise on its far shoulder. Large dams glistened below. The residence was every bit the baronial mansion Travis Vella had described. It sat imposingly on raised foundations, two-storeyed, made of local stone and with a veranda and balcony wrapping around two sides. Some of the Italianate ornamentation was in need of restoration, but not so much that it detracted from its sheer gobsmackingness.

The garden wasn't completely abandoned but light-years from the manicured perfection of its designer's vision. An original stone stable block, set to one side at a distance, contained several open-fronted bays where Elliot Claymore's

Jag was housed. The farm workhorse, a one tonner tray-top ute, was parked on the gravel forecourt. Rory pulled up alongside. He turned to Tahlia.

'It looks like this bloke I want to talk to is home. I'll try not to be long.'

Rory pressed the brass bell-press. No sound betrayed any cause and effect. He knocked, waited, then knocked again … louder. Nothing. He went back to the car, opened the driver side door and stooped to talk to Tahlia.

'I'll go check the outbuildings. You stay here.'

Rory disappeared around the side of the house.

Tahlia stepped from the car and took in the surroundings — the view across the valley, the house, the rambling old stable block. She wandered over. The open-fronted section was deep and not illuminated by windows. The gloom and dust gave a kind of blackness to everything, even the blue Jag. A workbench showed no sign of activity this side of the millennium. The surrounding grayscale of tools, light machinery and other discarded paraphernalia stretched back to one or other of the world wars, except for one particular item of colour that caught Tahlia's eye.

'WHAT THE FUCK ARE YOU DOING HERE?'

She spun around to see the 190-centimetre silhouette of Elliot Claymore. She opened her mouth to speak, but the figure had already begun striding purposefully towards her. A reasonable explanation wasn't going to cut it.

'WHO SENT YOU?'

He halted a metre short of Tahlia. Features of his face emerged as they adjusted to the dim interior. A life lived outdoors in rain, hail, and shine had grown the face into an exaggerated caricature. The nose and stray wires of nasal hair seemed to be taking over the whole show. Grey eyebrows had gone feral, and a stave of creases were planted across his forehead. A wide, rubbery lipless mouth was set between deep vertical valleys. Most petrifying were the pale eyes brimming with fury.

He grabbed her by an upper arm. His fist was accustomed to holding terrified sheep and cattle still while he crudely ministered doses of parasite control. It was a handhold from which there was no escape. The rigid loss of freedom gave Tahlia a voice.

'Let go of me, you fucking creep.'

She writhed impotently, confirming that his lock on her arm was welded on and he was not simply detaining her for a polite conversation. She kneed him in the groin. The blow landed, but with her arm locked tight, she hadn't got her weight behind it. Taking wind from his sails merely ramped the rage. He slapped her with unchecked force using his spare dinner-plate-sized hand. It sent her flying backwards against the bench. An explosion of pain ricocheted from the slapped side of her face to the other side of her face as it slammed against the bench. Somehow, the stink from a patina of baked-on engine oil managed to penetrate the blazing hurt as she slid to the floor.

She lifted herself on an elbow and felt for the blood on her face. *Some, but not too copious*, she was still able to reason … and nothing was broken. Her survival mode was surviving. *Still in one piece, so no sense hanging around*. She eyed the open ground she could run to beyond his legs.

'I'm sick of you people lurking around here again. We knew how to deal with your lot then, and I know how to deal with it now. If you're so keen to be here, you can join the last one who had the nerve to wander onto the place.'

She darted to his left. His hand shot out to grab her ankle, as easily as he might thwart a fit young wether making a break for it in the drafting yards. Her hand came out to try and stop her face from grinding into the hard dirt floor.

'Aaaaaaagh.' He retained his grip on her ankle to drag her from the shed. She struggled on her forearms to keep her face from dragging in the dirt.

'Aaaaaaaaagh'

'LET HER GO!'

Elliot Claymore turned askance to face Rory with a pistol raised to shoulder height and pointing at his head.

'Who are you?'

Tahlia sobbed as Claymore continued to hold her ankle with his hand vice.

'POLICE. LET GO NOW'.

Elliot Claymore glared unflinchingly. Rory fired. Deliberately aimed over his shoulder. The bullet clanged on something metal within the shed. Elliot Claymore let go.

'Hands behind your back.'

He put his hands behind his back … slowly. Suddenly he was laconic rather than rageful. Happy for the process to take longer than it should.

'Turn around.'

It was a slow turn.

'It's easy to see whose side you're on,' he told Rory.

Rory cuffed him to the nearest secure rail — the handle on a mammoth antique air compressor. He holstered his weapon and reached for Tahlia.

'Are you alright? Can you get up?'

'Ugh, I think.'

He helped her up and helped her teeter to the car. He sat her on the wide steps leading to the front door and fetched his water bottle from the car. She drank.

'I'll get something to bath the wounds.'

Tahlia nodded. Numbness setting in.

He went through the unlocked front door and came back with warm water in a basin and a white pillow slip. He cleaned Tahlia's face and forearms.

'I'll phone this in now and get you an ambulance.'

Tahlia pointed toward the shed.

Elliot Claymore was lurching away from the shed like a wounded bull, dragging a bung air compressor attached to one of his wrists.

'Fucking hell. Let him wear himself out. I'm making the call.'

Chapter 22

Michelle rang the doorbell. The chime was on the wall behind the door and clearly audible to the bell presser. She waited, then knocked.

'RORY, IT'S MICHELLE.'

She knocked again. This time giving the prolonged and heavy police knock.

'RORY. I KNOW YOU'RE IN THERE. OPEN UP.'

She gave another solid round of knocking, then tried a softer approach.

'Come on, Rory. Let me reciprocate.'

She allowed a half nano second pause.

'I'm not going away this time.'

She was going to give it five minutes but lasted two. Bang, bang bang bang bang.

'Come on, Rory. I know you're there. I waited until I saw the pizza guy come and go.'

She hadn't, but it was worth a try.

'Okay. That's it. If you don't come out this time, I'm breaking the door down. I've got the battering ram here.'

Another wait.

'I'm not kidding.'

'Last chance, Rory. I'll count to ten.'

She turned to a solidly built bald guy with his hands resting on the end of the instrument of the moment. Basically, a closed heavy metal tube with handles.

'You right, Bruno?'

'You sure? You sure he's in there?'

'I'm sure.'

'Then stand back.'

Bruno took two seconds to position himself, then took a backswing. BANG. The door exploded from its locking mechanism.

Michelle raced in. Rory was sitting almost prostrate on his couch. He peered at them through barely open eyelids and slurred:

'Jesus. Keep it down. You woke me up.'

'You right then?' Bruno asked Michelle.

'Yeah. Thanks, Bruno. I'll fix you up later.'

'"Fix me up?" I hope not, but opening the door is on me. I'll see myself out. I know the way now.'

She managed a reluctant smile at his humour, and he left. Michelle turned back to Rory. His eyes were closed again to resume sleep. The coffee table betrayed his diet of the last couple of days. Pizza and Absolut vodka. She lifted his feet to lay him lengthways on the sofa and fetched his doona. Then she set about tidying the place up and wondering how the door could be fixed. It was still on its hinges, but the lock had been busted out of the door. The lock-side jamb was a splintered mess. At least the security chain hadn't been in place when Bruno made his entrance. She could use that to keep the door relatively secure, if not entirely closed. She made herself a cup of tea and settled in for the long haul. Reciprocation via break-and-enter.

He woke to find Michelle asleep on duty in the lounge chair. He bumped his way along the short hallway to the toilet. If that didn't wake Michelle, then the sound of him urinating into the toilet water in the dead of night, with the door wide open, did.

Light through the kitchen door sliced into the lounge. Michelle waited. His silhouette appeared in the doorway, slouched against the jamb.

'Where's the Absolut?'

'No, Rory.'

'You haven't got rid of it, have you? Breaking and entering. Now theft? Why don't you just fuck off.'

His speech was slowed in a battle to remain coherent.

'I'm not going anywhere, Rory.'

'Oh Fuck.' He grabbed his head. 'What did you do with my Fentanyl?'

'Is that what they were?'

'Jesus, Michelle. You didn't?'

'You're not having anything until we talk about this.'

Rory dropped his head.

'This is not a PTSD thing you can intervene and pontificate about in your book. No nightmares. No flashbacks here. This is just me being a complete fuckhead. Just let me get on with it.'

He looked at his watch.

'It's six-thirty in the morning. The bottle shops don't open until nine,' she told him.

'Uuuuurh.'

He stumbled back to the couch and threw himself under the doona — entirely. She thought about her next move.

'You're not being a fuckhead, Rory.'

He lifted the doona off his face and found enough anger to prop his upper half up on an elbow.

'Oh no? I went to Kilmany specifically to dangle Tahlia in front of Claymore. That's what I did without telling her. I was the only one who thought that would be a good idea. How fucked up am I? I made that call without ever meeting Claymore. I had no idea what he was capable of. And I didn't tell her. She had no idea what she was walking into. She still has no idea why all that happened ... and I can't tell her.'

He paused to gulp with emotion.

'If that's not enough to live with ... how did it all play out? It ended up with me in the exact position I was with Heidi, pointing a gun at a madman. I couldn't have re-created that if I tried ... and yet ... that's exactly what happened. Oh fuck. Tell me you've got the vodka somewhere. Is it in your car? Can you go and get it?'

'You can tell her. She wants you to tell her.'

Rory sat up.

'What do you mean, she wants me to tell her?'

'Something Cockburn said.'

'You saw Cockburn?'

'I had to find out if you were still alive. You weren't answering my calls or my knocks on your door. They're assuming it was too much for you, and you've granted yourself more "special leave". They don't like to speaketh the word PTSD.'

It was familiar ground for Rory too. He knew they'd keep clear.

'What did he say about Tahlia?'

'He said she's not talking to anyone about the assault. She said she'll only talk to you. Cockburn's pissed off at her because it's not helping their case against Claymore. He was bailed in no time flat. He said he thought she was an intruder, that she only got injured trying to get away from him.'

'Shit. Is that all they're going Claymore for? The assault? Not even aggravated? What about Gloria Vella? I don't suppose Cockburn said anything about Claymore and Gloria Vella?'

'I asked him.'

'What? So now he knows about our pillow talk. That I talked to you about a case.'

'Cockburn couldn't give a fuck about that. He'd be the first … if he ever manages to get another woman.'

'So, what did he tell you?'

'He and Bourke are assuming you came up with nothing. Claymore's never been on their radar for Gloria Vella's murder, and it looks like it's going to stay that way.'

'How more fucked up can it get? You probably know I fired a warning shot. I'll already be under investigation for discharging a firearm. Now, do you believe I'm a fuckhead?'

They took a while to sit and look at each other. The battle of wills continued in silence. Then ebbed, as wills lost edge.

'I've got Panadol,' Michelle said.

'That's not gonna touch the sides.'

'It's a start. You've got work to do. You owe Tahlia something. If you don't tell Tahlia what's going on, I will. Cockburn also said you had a call from someone named Gaynor.'

He let Michelle's words sink before shrugging a kind of surrender. She knew, even if he had no talk left in him. He lay down on the lounge again and pulled the doona up. Michelle went to the kitchen and returned with a glass of water and the Panadol. She nudged him.

'Here. Take these. When you wake up, I'll still be here. We'll get you showered, coffee-ed and some bacon and eggs.'

He gulped the Panadol, looked at the nearly-closed front door and paused to say something before slumping back under the doona.

'I've been thinking. Now might be a good time for me to give you a key to my place.'

Chapter 23

Most sorry. I should have been in touch before now.
Important I speak to you, go over stuff in person. Will
text again in a few days to let you know where. Really
hope you can be there.
Rory.

Chapter 24

Tahlia stood at the waist-high cairn and scanned the moon-lit horizon. A torch light blinked roughly to the north. Perhaps a hundred metres more. She hunched into her puffy jacket and scrambled through boulders and heath. Rory was waiting for her on the lip of a rocky escarpment that fell to the plain. When the sun rose, the view before them would stretch 200 kilometres, encompassing an arc from Mount Buninyong at Ballarat to the Wimmera's Stick-Shed in Murtoa — that is, according to the brass disc embedded on top of the cairn. Of course, daylight would also illuminate the remaining 180 degrees of view westward from Mount William, the highest point of the Grampians.

'I was hoping you'd make the early shift,' Rory said.

'Sunrise from Mount Duwil, how could I resist, even with a forty-minute hike up the path to the top … in the dark. Mount Duwil's the Indigenous name, by the way.'

'I like it up here with no one around at this hour. Something like this, all to yourself.'

'You need that.'

It wasn't a question. She was telling him.

'I was hoping you'd come, full stop,' he said. 'After everything that happened, you've got every right to avoid me like the plague.'

She ignored his fishing for absolution.

'Hey, it's freezing up here. Can you fire that thing up?'

She nodded to the tiny gas hike-stove and billy. He'd come prepared. He soon had a blue flame bursting into a steady roar beneath a stovetop coffee pot. He retrieved two enamelled cups from his daypack and positioned them on the flat sandstone boulder. The sun began to show, not in a ball but in a glowing ribbon across the almost perceivable curvature of the earth. They sat shoulder to shoulder on the rock ledge and watched the glow set fire to a thin band of cloud hovering above the horizon.

'We're doing better than Major Mitchell, you know,' Tahlia said.

'Oh yeah?'

'You probably know he was the first European explorer to come this way.'

'I have heard. But isn't that history a bit too recent for an archaeologist?'

'Not at all; it all adds context. Anyway, the Major and his buddies wanted to climb up here and survey the way ahead because this is the highest point. They left their horses down there and came straight up the steep side. It took them so long;

the sun was setting when they reached the top. They had to spend the night, unprepared, to get the view in the morning. Right here, like we're doing now, only in the middle of winter. The night was so cold that sticks hanging out of their fire had icicles forming on the other ends. The health of two of his men suffered so badly from the cold, they never recovered normal strength.'

'Fuck.'

'To make matters worse, there was too much cloud around in the morning for him to do a proper survey. He did, however, discover these short-arse snow gums growing on the higher ground. Just in case you needed proof that this can be one of the coldest places in the state.'

'And look what he missed,' Rory said.

The sun's glow in the eastern sky had spread to the point where blue would begin to take over for the rest of the day. The coffee gurgled loudly as it escaped under pressure to the pot's upper chamber. Rory filled both cups and produced a muffin each.

Neither spoiled the moment with talking until the cosmic dimmer switch was cranked back to normal.

'Brill,' Tahlia finally offered.

'Even better than yesterday,' Rory responded.

Tahlia turned to him inquiringly.

'I figured if I have to get on top of all the stuff happening around here, then it might help if I was on top of it physically. What better place than the roof of the Grampians. And isn't the roof the traditional place that fuck-ups go to sort themselves out? … Well, you know. I guess none of this is a surprise to you after what I put you through.'

'I must be too young to know about the roof thing. But you don't owe me anything,' Tahlia said.

'You might think otherwise when I tell you what I'm about to tell you.'

She looked at him, ready to hear what he had to say.

'It was no accident that I took you to Elliot Claymore's property. Remember I told you that Ricky had become interested in Aboriginal massacres that took place around here? What I didn't tell you was that Cecil Gaynor, who I also mentioned to you, told Lenny Dalton about a hitherto unknown massacre he'd become aware of, carried out at Claymore's run by Claymore's ancestors. It was mentioned in old family correspondence Cecil had come across. Cecil and Lenny actually approached Elliot Claymore about it. They soon found he was less than appreciative of the idea, and they were unceremoniously sent packing. Not surprisingly, considering they were accusing Elliot Claymore's forebears of being mass-murderers. Not long after, the old letters Cecil had extrapolated his theory from were lost in a fire. As far as Lenny Dalton was concerned, that was supposed to be the end of that.'

'Supposed to be?' Tahlia was quick to ask.

'I found out from Ricky's uni mate, Leona, that Ricky probably contacted Cecil after that. That's all I know. Because Ricky was interested enough in the unrecorded massacre story to seek Cecil out, it might not be drawing such a long bow to imagine, you know … that he learnt enough to end up on

Claymore's doorstep. It was just a thought. I didn't have any evidence … and Cecil has since died.'

'Oh,' Tahlia said quietly and crossed her arms in a brace from the cold.

'Having told you all that, officially, my visit to Elliot Claymore wasn't about Ricky. It was about the Gloria Vella case. You realise she was the woman wrapped in the blue tarp?'

Tahlia nodded, and Rory continued.

'I was checking him out because he had acrimonious dealings with her husband, Travis Vella, when Gloria went missing. Believe it or not, in my mind, if not in Cockburn's, Claymore is a suspect for Gloria Vella's murder as well as having a possible link to Ricky's disappearance.'

He paused to allow that to sink in.

'When it turned out that you would be with me when I visited Claymore, I thought, if Ricky had ever been there, which was only a possibility in my head, then perhaps Claymore might react if he spotted you. I mean, assuming there's a family likeness … Look, I fucked up big time. I'm really sorry. I've made a few massive fuck ups in my lifetime that I'd change in a heartbeat and this one's right up there.'

He turned to the fading sunrise and shook his head.

She waited for him to turn back to her before she spoke.

'Well, aren't you glad it wasn't a waste of time?'

'What d'ya mean?'

'He murdered Gloria Vella, and he's responsible for whatever happened to Ricky.'

'We don't know any of that. That's the tragedy of this thing happening to you.'

'Stop being so miserable about it, and let me tell you. Firstly, before Claymore came at me, I saw a roll of rope in his shed. The same as the rope that was tied around the blue tarp that Gloria Vella was wrapped in.'

'Really?'

'Really. And secondly, when Claymore was getting stuck into me, this is what he said … as closely as I remember. "*I'm sick of you people lurking around here again. We knew how to deal with it then, and I know how to deal with it now. If you're so keen to be on my property, you can join the last one who had the nerve to wander onto the place*". It's not too hard for you and me to work out what he's talking about … is it?' Rory studied her face before answering.

'I didn't think your face looked too bad in the dark. Now that it's daylight … he made a real mess of you, didn't he? It'd be nice to think it wasn't in vain.'

'Don't worry about my face. It's fairly superficial, and I should mend quickly. What are you going to do?'

Rory looked back to the view. The man-made Lake Bellfield nestled between the ranges around Halls Gap. Oddly, the town was not visible from such a close and commanding prominence. To the north and east, other lakes glistened on the plain — the former Murray Basin inland sea — now a rich source of mineral sands that brought Travis Vella to this neck of the woods. He thought of Ricky and the nineteenth-century massacres — somewhere behind him where the view extended west across the Grampians — to the Victoria Range and beyond. If he was searching for context, he was in the right place.

'Don't tell me you didn't think any of this.' Tahlia added as Rory thought.

'What you just told me, it hasn't wrapped anything up and put a bow on it, but it gives me somewhere to take this. The rope? That particular kind of rope might be an unusual occurrence on a farm around there. It might not. As for what he said, he doesn't actually say what he might or might not have done. He could also deny saying it altogether.'

'Yeah, right. Why take the word of an Abo girl?'

'Hey. This is devil's advocate stuff. That's how you make a case bombproof. I learnt that Claymore was capable of all this stuff when I saw him lay into you. I don't need to be convinced. What I need is something I can work with to prove it. You've just given me that.'

He calmed a bit to add, 'You realise you'll need to make a statement at some stage?'

'That's okay. I climbed this mountain for you, didn't I?'

'More ...' The cogs kept turning in his brain. 'I've seen what's to see up here ... I think it's time to stop looking at sunrises.'

'In an hour. I reckon we've got the place to ourselves for at least that long. That coffee you made hit the spot. You got any more you can brew?'

Rory smiled. 'I've got a theory of why the coffee tastes better up here. We're over 1,000 above sea level. At this height, water boils at about ninety-six degrees rather than the usual one hundred. Coffee nuts insist that's the optimum temperature for optimum flavour.'

Tahlia pulled a suspicious face.

'Okay then, I've got enough for another brew, you be the judge.'

He set about making another brew.

'Where are you staying?' she asked.

'Jimmy's Creek Camping ground. I pitched a tent.'

'Wow. How is it there?'

'Pretty enough, but there was a shower of rain overnight and the tent leaked. My sleeping bag's soaked.'

'So, motel tonight.'

'Yep.'

By unanimous silence, small talk was done. Both were satisfied to be pre-occupied drinking coffee brewed at ninety-six degrees, looking and listening to birds, and a sharp breeze break the quiet. Faint chatter of day-trippers eventually rose from somewhere well down the summit path behind them. When they stood and turned to leave, their view south was marred by the silent march of technology.

'Shame about these telecommunications towers.'

Tahlia shrugged.

Before their descent, they checked out the Major Mitchell cairn with its 360-degree horizontal brass disc of pointers to places of interest.

'Not much rates a mention to the west.' Rory observed.

Tahlia pointed in that direction.

'The skyline over there is the Victoria Range. I looked up that massacre since you told me about it. There's also a few blanks to fill in beyond the Victoria Range.'

'I'm working on it.'

'You know the Major came down off the mountain empty-handed … without his precious survey info. I hope your sojourn has been more fruitful.'

'Not empty-handed. Not by a long shot.'

Chapter 25

From the Mount William carpark, Rory followed Tahlia back to Halls Gap, then continued on to Horsham. It was a one-hour drive, mostly along the highway from Melbourne to Adelaide. Somewhere beyond the Big Koala at Dadswells Bridge, the roadside forest gave way to the Wimmera plains — open wheat-land of unbounded shimmering flatness, stretching to the South Australian border and beyond.

Horsham soon loomed — a modern city by design. In a ruthless post war quest for modernism, most grand architecture it amassed over the previous one-hundred years was reduced to rubble and a signboard saying "Bert the Wrecker Was Here". The town's handful of historic two-storey pubs suffered a fate almost as brutal for the same cause. They all had their imposing shady verandas and balconies compulsorily stripped from them. The town had a lot of things going for it, but a stately past was no longer one of them. The metropolis of the Wimmera's post-war trajectory also sucked the life out of smaller towns within cooee and beyond. By default, it became the retirement village of choice for farmers, like Cecil Gaynor … and his still-living widow Marjorie.

The sat-nav took Rory to a growing riverside housing estate. To an unremarkable single-storey rendered home in a curved street of comparable display-centre designs. Marjorie's version had three healthy rose bushes alongside the narrow patch of lawn.

Rory was surprised to find the eighty-something-year-old's home was kitted out with thoroughly modern furnishings. He had entered a contemporary showpiece.

'That's because we lost everything when our farm house burnt down,' Marjorie explained. 'We decided it was time to move into town and built this with the insurance money. Cec passed the day before we were due to move in.'

'I was sorry to hear he died,' Rory said.

'Thank you … it's been a few years now.' Marjorie nodded. Not sure what more to say, she pressed on. 'Most of this furniture was in the display home. I loved it, and Cec didn't hate it too much, so we bought it.'

Marjorie reflected her penchant for modern with a fashionable tousle of shortish grey hair, a plain white top under a coat-length cardigan with pockets, a cluster of at least four modish necklaces and dangly earrings.

'How was it that you lost everything?'

'The house burnt to the ground. It happened in the middle of one day when we were both in town. We arrived home to a smouldering ruin. Quite literally. No one locally knew it was happening. No fire truck attended. It just caught alight somehow and eventually burnt itself out.'

'Do you know what caused the fire?'

'It was impossible to say, they said. Too much damage to tell.'

The jug switched itself off. She busied herself making tea. Once she had a cosy-clad pot and biscuits on the table, she got to the point without Rory's prompting.

'I got a call from Lenny Dalton. He told me about Ricky Lock and gave me your number to ring.'

'I'm sorry if I sounded a bit surprised. Lenny hadn't mentioned that Cecil was married,' Rory said.

'That's okay. I'm not sure I'll be able to help you though. And you've travelled so far.'

'I was up this way. It was easier to call in,' he reassured her. 'So, you know of Ricky. Can you tell me about that?'

'Yes. I met Ricky. He came to see Cec a few times. Initially, he came about the massacre stuff Cec had mentioned to Lenny. Then they got onto other local history stuff and could talk about it all day long. They hit it off.'

'What about the massacre information Cecil had unearthed. How did Ricky ...' Rory searched for a word, '... respond to that?'

'Well, I wasn't part of their conversations, although I'd often overhear them ... and sometimes Cec would relate things to me afterwards. I think Ricky was disappointed that Cec no longer had his great-great grandfather's letter about it. I know Cec gave his remembered account of events to Ricky ... for what that would have been worth. Also, I'm pretty sure

Cec also drew a mud map of where he thought the massacre took place. You see, that was the thing about the letter. Apparently, it included physical references that Cec recognised from the time he spent visiting the area in his youth. He thought he knew exactly where his great-great grandfather was referring to.'

'You mean Ricky had a hand-drawn map of where Cecil thought the massacre took place?'

'That's right.'

'Do you have a copy?'

'No. I'm certain he gave it to Ricky. I can tell you that wherever it occurred, it was somewhere on their neighbour, Claymore's, land. That much was clearly spelt out in the letter.'

'So, you actually saw the letter?'

'Oh, yes. A long while ago, though. I don't have a detailed memory of it like Cec did.'

Rory wasn't ready for a brick wall. Nor had Ricky been, he imagined.

'Do you know if Ricky's interest motivated Cecil in any way? Did they talk about visiting the site?'

'They did talk about that, but Cec wasn't at all keen, not after the letter had been lost in the fire. He was bitterly disappointed, but he understood the reality of making a claim with nothing to back it up. That was especially so when it concerned the Claymores. His and Lenny's encounter with Elliot Claymore troubled him, especially when Claymore followed it up with a letter from his lawyer. Cec told Ricky to leave it be.'

Rory stroked his chin. Room to move had just about vanished.

'Did Cecil ever think that his English relatives may have kept copies of the letters or scanned them onto genealogical websites? Anything like that?'

'Cec wasn't a computer person. He researched his family tree the old-fashioned way — through the mail and with some occasional help from the local genealogy association. Having said that, you've just reminded me that he decided to do exactly what you just said. To contact his English relatives to see if copies were ever made. I'd forgotten about that.'

She drifted off in thought as she said it, trying to conjure the memory.

'Maybe he didn't get around to doing it before he passed because no more correspondence ever arrived from them,' she added.

'Do you have those relatives' details?'

'I thought we'd get to this point. It's all in there.'

She slid a manilla folder across the table to Rory. It had been on the table when he arrived, and he'd taken no notice. Now that he *was* taking notice, it appeared slim enough to be empty.

'Everything Cec had went up in the fire. That's all he'd managed to re assemble. His relatives sent him copies of his family trees. Their contact details will also be in there … but not much else. You're welcome to have a look.'

'Thanks, Marjorie. I might photograph anything I need if that's all right.'

'That won't take you long. It seems so little after the mass of documents he painstakingly gathered researching those trees. The local history records he collected. It broke his heart.'

'You never know. Sometimes something small can make all the difference.'

Chapter 26

'You're back.'

Bourke had lifted his eyes from the screen and stopped typing an email. He leant back into his task chair, welcoming the interruption.

'Take a seat.'

Rory came from the office doorway and sat opposite Bourke.

'You okay now? You're looking okay.'

'Yeah. I'm good. No need to start writing reports about me. I just needed a break. I got back to work yesterday.'

'Hmm,' Bourke said, and nodded thoughtfully.

'You know the Conduct Unit want to speak to you about discharging your weapon?'

'I fired a warning shot. We were in the middle of nowhere, and he was refusing to release the girl he was harming. She was injured, in pain, and in danger. A warning shot did the trick.'

Bourke nodded more.

'Alright. I'll let them know you're back on deck. Now, where were you yesterday?'

'In Horsham.'

'Horsham? Doing what exactly?'

'Long story. Have you got time?'

'FRAN.'

His PA Fran appeared at the door. Fran was about the same "old school" age as Bourke. He felt safe enough to push advances in equal opportunity.

'Can you go down and buy Rory and me a real coffee without someone from HR learning that I asked you to?'

Fran rolled her eyes and set off.

Rory told his long story. He only paused for Fran to deliver their coffees.

'Jesus, Rory. You've got the same bloke in the gun for both cases. Have you told Cockburn about this yet? He's just about got Travis Vella tried and convicted, you know?'

'I'll tell him after this. I just wanted to bounce it off someone without the histrionics.'

'Who's to say you won't get the histrionics from me. It sounds to me like some dumb-arse lord-of-the-manor throwback who would have no idea the woman in Sydney he's supposed to have knocked off existed. How would he even know where such a total stranger to him lived? From what you say about Travis Vella's job, he and his wife are not gonna be listed in the phone book. Nor is the Luddite you tell me

Claymore is, going to track her down on social media. And all you've got so far is some rope that looks like the rope used to secure that blue tarp the body was wrapped in.'

'I know there's a lot of leg work to do. I'm just letting you know what I'll be working on. Don't forget Ricky Lock's car was hidden in the same bushland, within two kilometres of the gem site where Gloria Vella was buried. That might pass as a half-believable coincidence if it weren't for Claymore's name popping up for both.'

Bourke took a leisurely sip of his coffee.

'That fascinates me, I have to say. But it doesn't prove anything in itself, does it? I mean, there's no certainty Ricky Lock ever met Claymore. And we haven't established a crime regarding Ricky Lock. Still ...'

Rory welcomed the "Still ..." at the end of Bourke's sentence. One word was enough to know Bourke was at least open to the possibility.

'All of the above,' Rory acknowledged. 'I'll keep you posted.'

'... and Cockburn with the Gloria Vella case,' Bourke reminded him.

'Yep. I'll give him a heads up when you and I have finished. Do you know how he's going, honing in on Travis Vella?'

'Yeah. Natalie's retrieved what CCTV footage the New South cops collected last time round. Apparently, there's more than you'd expect. Natalie's also ahead of where they got to last time. She's got her hands on an app that enhances vehicle images on grainy CCTV footage and identifies the make and model. It's a prototype from a local start-up. They offered it to the force to road test. So far, it's brilliant. They've already got some white HiLux matches they're working through.'

'Sounds interesting,' Rory said. 'One other thing,' he added. 'A search warrant for Claymore's place?'

'What for? To retrieve a bit of rope? Forget it. Especially with the assault charges he's facing, yet to play out. There's no way I want those waters muddied. You've got a witness who said it's the same rope. Work with that unless you come up with something worthwhile.'

Rory took no for an answer.

'Alright. Now for the histrionics.'

Cockburn disappointed. He listened and then tried his version of a benevolent counsellor.

'You've excelled yourself, Rory. Lining up some cranky old sheep shagger, not only for one murder but also for another one we don't even know exists. So, it's lucky you came to me when you did. I can save you wasting a lot of your time. Show him, Nat.'

He got Natalie to bring up some of the four-plus-year-old CCTV footage on her screen. The first example she retrieved was at a roadhouse somewhere in New South Wales. It was grainy and black and white.

'Back then, Travis Vella was driving a white one-year-old Toyota HiLux with some of those built-in tradie tool cabinets on the back. A single cab. No signage.' Natalie explained. 'At the time, there was more low-definition black and white CCTV systems around like this. Especially if you chose to fill

240

up at one of the smaller independent petrol outlets. The daytime footage is half usable, but the nighttime stuff is shit, that is until you apply the Vehicle Knowall — our new targeted-enhancement app. Watch this.'

She let the tape roll in slow motion as a white one-tonner-shaped blur arrived at a petrol pump.

'With this black and white footage, we're lucky the vehicle he drove was white. It'd be much more of a struggle with anything coloured. Now, what brand do you reckon that is?'

Rory leant forward, knowing he'd be none the wiser.

'Nah. Could be anything.'

Natalie used the mouse to position a yellow square border tightly around the white blur. She clicked. The vehicle instantly became a sharply defined single cab four-wheel-drive ute, albeit a model unrecognisable in the small mid-screen inset on a wider, blurry black and white view. She clicked again, and the sharp inset filled the screen. The vehicle was recognisable as a Ford Ranger. If the viewer was in any doubt, the application superimposed the vehicle year, make and model on the screen.

'Wow. Very impressive,' Rory said. 'What's the accuracy?'

'Ninety something percent, apparently', Natalie replied. 'It's slow work, but we've had a few HiLux matches so far. We've been able to eliminate a few of those where the servo operators have kept their Eftpos records from that long ago. That allowed us to link the vehicle and the payment by the corresponding time. Cash payments are useful too because they flag no-card users like Vella would have been.'

Cockburn was also keen to talk up Natalie's new toy.

'Yeah, Rory. If I were you, I wouldn't waste my time with this Claymore shit. This is the perfect weapon to nail Vella. Leave it to Natalie. She's all over this footage. Even when it comes to the super low-definition systems a few of the residences had in Travis Vella's neighbourhood.'

'Nice work, Natalie,' Rory said.

Cockburn wasn't done.

'As for your little cultural-awareness buddy — who sounds like she's trying to hang it on Claymore for revenge — tell her they'll have no trouble doing him for assault. See if that gives her some comfort. Any influential old-boy legal network Claymore thinks he can plug into died out years ago. He mightn't end up inside, but he'll cop a decent fine or even a community corrections order. That'll hurt someone like that.'

'Exactly like it'd happen if their roles were reversed,' Rory said.

Chapter 27

Rory arrived at his flat to find his battered front door with a temporary latch, and padlock securing it to the splintered jamb had all been replaced. The whole box and dice had been replaced with a brand-new unpainted set. He took a step back and looked left and right along the walkway as if expecting the culprit to be standing around, or at least a sniggering prankster.

He studied the door and nodded approvingly. It had a keyhole and a handle but no knob to turn. He tried his old key. It wouldn't even enter the keyhole. *Fuck* formed silently on his lips as he studied his set of keys hopelessly. He tried knocking.

The sound of approaching movement within emanated, then the sound of the locking mechanism turning. The door swung open to reveal a smug Michelle.

'What do you think?'

Rory shook his head disapprovingly. 'I would have got there.'

'It wasn't your responsibility.'

'That's debatable.'

He stepped over the threshold and kissed her … well. When they parted, she held out her hand.

'Here are the new keys.'

Rory took the keys and looked at them.

'I'm supposed to be giving you a key to my place, not the other way round,' he said.

'I kept one for myself. The other one on the keyring is to my place.'

'Oh. So, I guess we are an item then.'

'In our world, I don't think not knocking each other's doors off their hinges is setting the bar too low. So I guess we are something … if you're game.'

He looked at the keys as if he'd just learnt they were forged from gold, then kissed her again. Longer this time.

'Thanks,' he said, holding the keys in his upturned hand as if trying to estimate their weight. 'Are you going to hang around? I've got pizza coming.'

'So have I. I rang it through when I saw you drive in.'

'You're joking. Mine's capricciosa, from Carlisle Pizza.'

'No way …' She had made the same call.

'Well, we won't be dying of hunger. I think I should crack us a beer.'

The news played on the television in the background as they sat at the table eating capricciosa pizza and beer.

'You're on Facebook, aren't you?' Rory asked Michelle.

'Of course. I can't afford not to be in my game. I know you're not on Facebook, though. Why do you ask?'

'Have a look at this and tell me what I need to do.'

Rory slid his phone from the other side of the table and opened a text message.

> Dear detective. Lucas Curry turned up on Facebook this week. He has been out of mob phone range at Mexican ruins. Still in Mexico but now near wifi. Told him about you reviewing Ricky's case. Says he can speak to you if you contact him on Facebook. He might know stuff I don't. Leona.

'Leona and Lucas. Are they the uni mates Ricky went with to Halls Gap?'

'Yeah.'

'Can I answer this text for you?' Michell asked.

'I think you'd better.'

Michelle did the two thumbs typing.

> Thanks Leona. I'm not on Facebook, but my friend Michelle Fox Jones is happy for me to contact Lucas using her Facebook account. Can you please let Lucas know that I will organise to do so over the next few days. Looking forward to talking to Lucas.
> Rory.

She slid the phone across to Rory.

'Press Send if you're okay with it.'

He glanced down and pressed Send as quickly as he read it.

'Anything else I can help you with?' she took pleasure in saying.

'I've got a job I'd love to hand over to you … if only I could. I've spent the day trying to trace the rope used to wrap Gloria Vella's body. Trying to track down suppliers and distributors for a particular kind of rope they stopped importing into the country almost ten years ago. A lot of the suppliers don't exist anymore. Still, I've been able to track down where and when Claymore probably purchased a bundle. To make the job harder for myself, I discovered that a bundle or two turned up at a farm clearing sale in later times. It's shaping up as pretty bloody unlikely, but …'

He paused to extract a ray of hope from what he had just said.

'… by definition, "unlikely" means the adverse is possible.'

'You sound like you're ignoring the possibility that Travis Vella could have bought the same rope … or acquired it by some other means,' Michelle said.

'I'm in denial and letting Cockburn worry about that. This is hard enough as it is.'

'I'd love to help, but this hair isn't going to wash itself. Ask me an easier one.'

'Alright then. Tell me this: You're old. You're a Luddite that doesn't have a mobile phone. You want to find out someone's address, and all you know is that they come from New South

Wales — their vehicle has New South Wales number plates — and they're not listed in the phone book.'

Michelle bit the pointy end off another slice of pizza and stared blankly as she chewed.

'The electoral roll?'

'Possible, I suppose. But you'd have to visit an electoral commission office, and he wouldn't want to leave a trail. I think the nearest one would be a couple of hours away. I don't think it's likely.'

'Then it was written on a piece of paper for him.'

This time Rory chewed and thought.'

'Sorry. It's the best I can come up with,' Michelle apologised.

'No. That's exactly what might have happened. It was already written down for him.'

He waited for Michelle to leave his flat in the morning, then made a mental calculation in his head. "*Six*". It was the number of times they'd spent the entire night together — including Dunkeld, but not counting the night each spent responding to the other's meltdown. *Not bad*, he decided in his head and wondered: *Will I stop counting when we reach double figures? Was Michelle counting too?* An answer came: *We're still together, so stop analysing it.*

He dialled Travis Vella. Travis was surprised to hear from Rory.

'*Detective James. Not someone I expected to call.*'

'I imagine not. Where are you? Have you got a moment?'

'*I was driving on a sandy red track in the Mallee. I pulled over to take this call.*'

'And you're on your own?'

'*Yep. What's it about?*'

'I'm just ringing for some detail about your interactions with Elliot Claymore. When you went back to apologise for entering his property without permission.'

'*Oh yes …*' Travis said, sounding sceptical.

'I went to Kilmany to see him the other day. It made me think of something you said when you told me about your encounter. You began by saying to me, "When I finally found him". What did you mean by that?'

'*I said that because I had phoned and arranged a time to meet him at his house. He didn't answer the door when I got there, even though his car and ute were there. I went wandering about the place, trying to find him. Checked the machinery sheds, the woolshed and all that. After I gave up and went back to my ute, there he was, standing there waiting for me.*'

'You phoned and arranged the meeting beforehand?'

'*Yeah, I would have phoned him on the landline because he didn't have a mobile back then … I don't know about now. I would have phoned him early evening, the traditional time for catching a farmer in the pre-mobile phone era. We arranged to meet the following morning. He said he'd hang around the homestead until I came.*'

'What happened exactly when you arrived? I presumed you parked on the forecourt at the front of the house.'

'*I did.*'

'And he didn't come to the door when you knocked?'

'*No. Like I said. I went around the back to the outbuildings to try and find him.*'

'Okay. So, when you get back to your ute. He's standing there waiting. He hasn't come looking for you?'

'*No.*'

'And your ute wouldn't have been locked.'

'*Of course not. But I don't think I would have left the keys in it. And he couldn't have stolen anything. We cart all our gear in the locked tradie cabinets on the tray. The same as my current setup; you would have seen that when I called to see you.*'

'Yeah. I remember. What about inside the cabin?'

'*There would have been nothing of real value. A hi-vis jacket maybe, my lunchbox, a mining journal or two ... you stuck your nose in and saw what it was like when I came to Melbourne.*'

'I did.'

'*So, what does all this have to do with anything?*'

'I'm intrigued that he allowed you to come and see him even though, from what you told me, he wasn't interested in your apology.'

'*No. I think he just wanted an opportunity to have a go at me. To put the wind up me by telling me, "I would suffer like he did". Whatever that was supposed to mean. Anyway, what happened when you went to see him?*'

'I'm afraid I didn't get to speak to him about you because, while I was there, he assaulted a Parks Victoria officer who was travelling with me. A woman.'

'*What? He assaulted a woman?*'
'Yeah. He's been charged with assault.'
'*Well, now you know what I'm talking about.*'

Chapter 28

Rory wandered out to Michelle's kitchen in his boxers and tee shirt. Michelle, in her own random version of PJs, had already fired up her laptop.

'Three AM. Is this the best you could do?'

'Don't put it on me. I didn't put Mexico where it is. Do you want a Milo? I've got the jug on.'

'Buggered if I know. Is that what people do at this hour? I've gone to bed this late but never got up this early … unless I'm busting.'

'Well, you'd better go and put a comb through your hair, at least. We're doing this on Video Chat.'

'Fuck.'

He trudged to the bathroom.

'Didn't you comb your hair?' Michelle asked when he came back. Rory pulled a pained face. She handed him a cup of Milo.

'See if this helps. I'm going to start.'

Michelle sat Rory down in front of the laptop and reached in to operate the touchpad. She brought up Lucas Curry's icon and clicked the video camera symbol. She was ready to wait for a period of dial-tone, but the sound of a packed, small outdoor dining area burst into the room. Rory jolted. The face of a twenty-something, backpacking archaeologist grinned back at him. Suntanned, with several weeks of new-beard growth. His hair rivalled Rory's for just-out-of-bed recalcitrance.

'Hey, man.'

'Hey,' Rory found himself replying. 'Thanks for doing this.'

The perimeter wall behind Lucas was horizontal corrugated iron stencilled with coloured variants of an intensely Mexican design. The table he sat at was one of several weathered park table/seat combinations in view, brought alive with the hi-vis decorated Calavera — a kind of cartoon skull — and an array of equally dazzling food, drinks and condiments.

'This is Sandy,' Lucas shouted over the hubbub of diners, music and highway noise. Sandy leant in and said, "Hi," and her hair fell over her face.

'Hi, Sandy,' Rory said. 'Where are you guys?'

He got the long answer.

'We're back in Ensenada. It's not that far across the US border. We set out to see the coneheads at Sonora, but it wasn't happening, man, so we went deeper, all the way down to Yaxchilan and Bonampak. That blew us away.'

'It looks like the middle of the day over there. What time is it?' Rory wondered aloud.

'It is, man. It's lunchtime. That's why we're here. This is Taqueria Criollo. The best fucking seafood tacos in Mexico. That's cool, isn't it? Swearing to a policeman. The thing with Criollo is, a young surfer chef dude from California and his chef woman started it. Like, they're not even Mexican. Mexica-pop, they say. If you ever come here, order the shrimp. They pile shrimp — did I say Ensenada is a fishing port and the shrimp's as fresh as — and all this crazy tasting salad stuff on a fried taco with mashed spud filling. Kind of an Aussie touch. Maybe that's why I dig 'em.'

He took a breath.

'It probably sounds great, mate, when it's not three o'clock in the morning. Can I ask you about Ricky?'

'Sorry man, I didn't realise it would be three o'clock there. Is that why you've got the cool hair thing happening? You should'a called earlier … or later. Maybe you need to have one of these iced coffees.'

Rory shot a scowl at Michelle.

'So, what can I tell you about Ricky?'

'Thanks, mate. I'm trying to find out about Ricky and Cecil Gaynor. That's the name of the old bloke who told Ricky about the unknown massacre. Did Ricky mention any of that to you?'

'Shit, yeah. He went on about it all the time. The old dude drew him a map of where he thought it went down. Ricky wanted someone to go there with him. I gave it a miss. I think he also asked Leona, and she gave it a miss too. We'd already gone with him to look for the site of a massacre they did have on the books, but unless you've got some good intel, that game's a dead loss.'

'Did he show you the map?'

'Yeah. He had it. But I can't recall any detail for you, man. Not now.'

'Do you know if Ricky went there?'

'He didn't say to me, "I'm going there now", and wave goodbye to me, like. But I reckon he would have went, even if he had to go alone. I don't think he would have died wondering.'

Sandy's elbow came onto the screen to nudge him hard.

'Oh fuck. Did I say that, man? Sorry.'

He bit his lip and shook his head before continuing.

'It's freaking me out that that could be connected to Ricky going missing. I could'a done something. We could have gone with him, man. Me and Leona.'

'Don't go there, Lucas. We don't know what happened to Ricky yet. This is just one line of inquiry. Okay.'

'Okay.'

The talking machine stopped. Sandy's hand came into view to comfort him on the shoulder.

'I'll go get you a beer, babe,' she said.

The laptop speakers were reduced to the Mexican version of silence, the suddenly eerie restaurant hubbub. Lucas felt the silence first.

'Anything else I can tell you, man? Anything to help Ricky.'

Rory scratched his three AM brain with both hands, wracking it for something else to ask.

'What are the coneheads?'

Michelle looked dumbstruck. It brought Lucas back to life.

'Oh, wow, man. These are like thousand-year-old skeletons they dug up that have actual cone skulls. Just like the sci-fi movie, only they're real humans. Maybe twenty or more of them. We were so bummed we couldn't check out the dig or see one. You should check it out on YouTube yourself. These things are so radical ...'

Sandy arrived with their beers.

'Thanks, Babe. You know what? We should try again to see the coneheads before we leave the land of blue agave. What d'ya think?'

'I might leave you guys to ponder that important question. Thanks for chatting, and enjoy the rest of your travels,' Rory said.

They wound things up, and Michelle reached in to end the connection.

'You want to go back to bed, man?' Michelle said.

'Yeah, babe.'

Chapter 29

Rory watched Natalie methodically inch some grainy black and white footage on to the next white ute shape; position the square cursor over the blurry outline and bring it into focus; repeat the process until one of the shapes happened to be a HiLux; record the details of time and place; then add it to a mounting list to be followed through with a further mountain of tracing and checks.

'Still at it?' he said. 'I thought you'd be well and truly done by now.'

''Tis the exciting life of a homicide policewoman. Can't you tell I'm addicted to it? I dream about it every night.'

Rory ignored the sarcasm.

'Any success yet?'

'NO! … sorry, Rory. Every fricken clown who wanders past me stops for a perv and asks me that.'

'I can see why it gets them in. It's kind of mesmerising. But I came with a purpose. Is there another copy of all that footage?'

Natalie stopped going through the motions and swivelled her chair to beam at Rory.

'Are you going to help then?'

'Sorry to disappoint. I want to check for something else.'

'And what might that be?' she said with the smile wiped from her face.

'A long shot.'

Natalie gave an exasperated sigh.

'This lot came on an external hard drive. Here, you take it. I'm sick of the fricken thing. You can bring it back tomorrow. I deserve a break.'

'You sure?'

'Take it. I can't give you the Vehicle Knowall app, but if you find anything interesting, earmark it, and I'll bring it up on *my* computer.'

Rory was only ten minutes into looking at the footage in his own office when he realised what a saint Natalie was to have stuck at it so long.

When his phone rang, and he pounced on it, it was Tahlia.

'*Any news with the things I told you about?*' she asked.

'I'm working on some of that stuff right now. Nothing to report yet. I also spoke to Lucas Curry, another archaeologist mate of Ricky's. He's in Mexico. He confirmed that Cecil Gaynor gave Ricky a hand-drawn map of where he thought the unrecorded massacre took place on Claymore's property. He also says Ricky was determined to go there and that he probably did go there … and probably on his own. At some point, we'll ask Claymore about it. I'm not at that point yet, though. There are still too many probables.'

'*Uh-huh.*'

Rory expected more.

'Don't worry. The wheels are turning,' he offered.

'*You realise Ricky's abandoned car and Gloria Vella's body were found within two kilometres of each other.*'

'That's why I'm working on it. I'm no archaeologist, but I imagine you also need to join a lot of dots to prove a theory, right?'

The phone line was quiet. Rory knew she had something to say.

'*Promise me one thing. When you do go back to Claymore's place, take me with you.*'

'What?'

That was something Rory didn't see coming.

'*There was something about the place. Something I felt as we were driving in ... before Claymore found me in his shed. You know that's something I can't leave hanging. I just can't. I have to go back.*'

'I don't know, Tahlia. Not with the charge pending for him assaulting you. You don't want that fucked up.'

'*Well, whenever. Promise you'll take me there when you can. I've been patient, and I can be patient for a bit longer. But you know I can't not see it through.*'

This time Rory took his time answering.

'Okay. I'll take you there … if and when we take Claymore in.'

He hit the wall before he'd spent an hour staring at video footage.

'This is all wrong,' he told his computer screen, closed the program and ejected the external hard drive. Within minutes he was back upstairs at Natalie O'Quinn's workstation.

'Not as easy as it looks, is it?' she greeted him.

'Correct me if I'm wrong, but everything in this collection of footage is only for Friday and part of Saturday on the weekend Gloria Vella went missing.'

'That's right. That's the window Travis Vella had to make a trip to Sydney.'

'Well, it's useless for finding someone doing that trip who wasn't restricted to Travis Vella's window … and yes, I realise the New South cops didn't have a body at that time, nor any other suspects in Victoria.'

'So?'

'What about neighbourhood residents' CCTV from where Gloria Vella lived? Wasn't there meant to be footage from a couple of those?'

'There is, but not in that lot. The hard drive I gave to you is a collection they gathered from a sweep of the main routes from Western Victoria to Sydney. They discovered the neighbourhood cameras later. That stuffs on a couple of DVDs in the package Gary collected in Sydney. It's pretty low grade and grainy, but it does cover the entire window for when Gloria went missing. I gather you'd like a look.'

'You read my mind.'

It took one hour and forty minutes for Rory to find a retro Jaguar burning oil — even without the enhancer app. He was back at Natalie's workstation in minutes. This time, Cockburn was there.

'Thanks for making an appearance, oh Spirit-of-Cold-Cases … and what are you looking so excited about?'

Rory held a DVD up and answered, 'CCTV footage from Gloria Vella's neighbourhood. Take it to the one hour, twenty-nine minute, thirty-two second mark Nat, and do your stuff with the Vehicle Knowall. Tell me what we've got.'

Natalie began loading the DVD.

'Don't tell me you fluked it. You got the prick's ute,' Cockburn said, not without some satisfaction.

'I've got *a* vehicle.'

'I'll tell you exactly what you've got,' Natalie said and clicked the mouse.

The app told them it was a 1976 Jaguar XJ Series 2. Cockburn leant in to see there was no mistake. The vehicle was clearly a sedan, one that was also clearly burning oil.

'What the fuck?'

'Can we do a vehicle search for Elliot Claymore,' Rory asked Natalie.

Cockburn continued to rail:

'OH FUCK OFF, RORY. What kind of long bow are you trying to draw here to make a point? This is bull-fucking-shit. TOTAL BULL-FUCKING SHIT. If you're going to pull stuff out of your arse, you can at least do it with something that nails Travis Vella. Who's fucking side are you on?'

Natalie had just as quickly brought up Elliot Claymore's vehicle registrations on screen. She pointed to the description. "1976 Jaguar XJ, Series 2".

'Fucking cute, Rory. You found a car the same as Claymore drives. So fucking what? Two cars of the same make a thousand miles apart. We know Claymore would never have known Gloria, let alone know where she lived. Get real.'

Bourke arrived to see what was going on.

'What's all this about?'

'I've just placed Elliot Claymore's car near Gloria Vella's house on the weekend she went missing. It's on home CCTV from one of her neighbours.'

'Really. Well, bugger me.' He leant in to check the image. 'And you have a problem with this, Gary?'

'Two cars of the same make. Whoever heard of such a thing?'

'Two cars of the same uncommon make, with Victorian number plates, and burning oil.' Rory countered Cockburn's sarcasm.

Cockburn and Bourke both leant even closer to see the Victorian number plate.

'Can you do anything to make it legible, Nat?' Bourke asked.

'This prototype of the app doesn't have number plate recognition, something to do with patents, I think. The best I can do is to zoom in.'

The numberplate gained no clarity in its enlarged form, but the blurred shapes of an "0" and an "I" or "1" could now be discerned … and they were in the correct relative positions.

'That looks pretty convincing to me. Ninety-five percent we're not looking at a different car,' Natalie concluded.

'What's going on, Rory. How did Claymore know where the Vella's lived?' Bourke asked.

'Travis Vella carries some of his mail and un-opened, addressed subscription copies of geo magazines in his ute. The last time he and Claymore met before Gloria Vella went missing was a catchup they arranged to take place at Claymore's homestead. Despite having made an appointment, Travis Vella had to wander around Claymore's outbuildings looking for him. When he couldn't find him, he returned to the house to leave, and there was Claymore waiting beside Vella's unlocked ute.

'And Claymore wouldn't be fazed by the prospect of having to drive to Sydney. That's where he met and courted his wife, Eva. She worked with a national woolgrowers' outfit up there when Claymore was a rep attending its board meetings. Assuming Percy Sledge knew what he was singing about, by the time they got married, Claymore's Jag could've driven itself to Sydney.'

'Okay. You lost me with Percy Sledge, but it stacks up. And his motive being …'

'He's a cranky and fierce bastard. It wasn't that long ago a similar sort of character bumped off a government land officer he took exception to for perceived interference with his farm. Apart from anything else, Claymore fits that profile to a tee.'

Bourke wondered aloud. 'Then why didn't he just knock off Travis Vella? Why go Vella's wife? Did he even know he had a wife?'

That was enough doubt for Cockburn to jump on the bandwagon. 'Yeah. I don't buy it, even if this is Claymore's car. This is still la la land.'

'I think he went after Vella's wife because he's smarter than people think. If he killed Vella, he knew he'd be a prime suspect after the mega run-in they had. He'd also just had his own wife walk out on him. Maybe he intended to inflict wife-less-ness on Vella. Maybe that's what he meant by his final words to Vella — "He'd make him suffer like he did".'

'According to Vella.' Cockburn said.

'That's right, but there is more to this. Something else he's covering up. You need to go in with a search warrant. Especially for that Jag. Remember, Gloria Vella died of asphyxia in a confined space. Try travelling all the way from Sydney in a car boot. We need to do the search warrant and get him in an interview room.'

Rory was looking at Cockburn. It was his case. He was angling for buy-in from Cockburn. Or at least a ceasefire.

'I agree. Do it, Gary,' Bourke said.

In his mind, Rory was ready for Bourke to give the okay.

'Don't drive the Jag. Put it on a flatbed and get it to forensics. If Gloria Vella was in the boot, there's been more than four years for traces to dematerialise. We can't afford to disturb a thing. The rope's important too. You never know; they might be able to tell if it's from the same spool. And can you make sure the warrant covers Claymore's entire landholding,' Rory said.

'Aren't you coming,' Cockburn asked.

'I intend to be around, but I want to leave it till after Claymore's been taken in … so I can take my time. Can you phone me when he's outta the way, please, Natalie?'

'Sure. Does this mean I can stop looking at this fricken pile of CCTV footage?' she pleaded.

'Hello, Travis Vella.'

'It's Rory James here. I need you to do something for me.'

'Sure. If it'll help.'

'The paddock that your offsider, Tony, did seismic work in without knowing it was part of Claymore's property.'

'You mean the one where Claymore sprung him and put an axe into our recorder?'

'That's the one. Do you remember exactly where it was? Could you show me on a map?'

'I could MMS one in the next half hour if it's important.'

'Let's assume it is then. Now. One other thing I might need your help with. Tell me about the ground-penetrating radar you use.'

Chapter 30

As ever, Tahlia was there before Rory. As he drove into the car parking area, he thought Tahlia had brought her mother along. Both were settled on a seat facing onto empty tennis courts beside the weatherboard country hall. Tahlia had found a shady tree for her car near the corrugated-iron toilets. She was in her Parks Victoria uniform.

As Rory walked from his car, he could see that the older woman was closer to being Tahlia's grandmother than her mother. She was nevertheless smooth-skinned for the age suggested by her copious silver hair, pulled back and tied high at the back of her head. She wore un-framed glasses and a long blue cardigan over an Aboriginal patterned shirt.

'Hi,' Tahlia greeted Rory. 'This is Beverly, she's been travelling with me today. I hope you don't mind if she comes with us. I don't want to leave her here. She's an elder who knows this country.'

'No. Of course. How are you, Beverly?'

'Good, thank you,' Beverly said with a gravitas that told Rory their conversation was over. Rory turned back to Tahlia.

'Shall we get going, then?' Tahlia said. Gravity had become the order of the day.

They took their places in Rory's car. Tahlia in the front seat, Beverly in the rear.

'I take it Claymore has been taken into custody ... again', Tahlia said.

Rory glanced at Beverly in the rear-view mirror before answering. He felt constrained in how freely he should converse with Tahlia.

'He's been taken in for questioning at this stage.'

'Uh-huh. Good.'

As he drove, Rory took a folded printout from his shirt pocket and handed it to Tahlia. It was a section of the map that covered all of the property in the Claymore holding. An "X" was marked in red on a paddock, two along from the long driveway to the house.

'What's the "X" for?'

'That's what Claymores calls "The She-oak paddock". I thought we'd go there first.'

'Why there?'

'I have my own feeling.'

Tahlia turned to fathom his profile as he drove.

They reached a nondescript gate opening onto the sealed public road. Tahlia did the opening and closing. Wheel ruts crossed the paddock to a second gate. There was no track in the grassed second paddock. Rory crossed the beginning of a gully then skirted around a large stand of mature she-oak trees. That the stand was original remnant vegetation was evident from the understorey of grass trees and a few she-oaks that had died of old age, now lying in various stages of decay.

As he rounded the end of the trees, Beverly reached forward and tapped Tahlia on the shoulder. Rory knew to stop.

They alighted. Rory and Tahlia held back and watched Beverly slowly pick her way through lush grass to where the land began to slope into a broad valley. Beyond Beverly, the slope was deeply scoured where the land had struggled with post-clearing water run-off. She came to a halt about 100 metres from the car. Tahlia went to her.

Rory watched the pantomime of Beverly pointing things out to Tahlia as a light breeze turned the she-oaks' needle foliage into soothing wind harps. He watched them put their arms around each other and stand a long time in sorrow.

Beverly carried her sadness back to the car and returned to the car seat.

'How does she know?' Rory asked.

'She just knows,' Tahlia answered.

'Can you show me where, so I can mark it,' Rory said.

'She thinks they fought amongst these trees, and they were buried over there. You can mark it if you want to, but you can't break the ground without due archaeological process.'

'I had something less invasive in mind.'

'What? Ground-penetrating radar?'

'I know a guy.'

'Really,' Tahlia said, quietly pleased. 'Then let's go and mark the site.'

Without saying anything, Tahlia grew edgy as they drove up the driveway. Before they reached the house, Rory was forced onto the grass verge to allow an oncoming tow truck to pass. Claymore's Jag was lashed to its tray. The truck was being followed by the forensic van and a marked police car. One other police vehicle and a uniformed officer were present when Rory parked in the grand forecourt of Kilmany mansion. It was five thirty.

'Wait here,' he said to Tahlia and Beverly.

Both watched Rory introduce himself to the officer charged with overnight security of the site. Rory explained that he was here to have a look inside the house. He might be a while. In the meantime, his passengers may want to stretch their legs. Could he keep an eye out and make sure they don't stray? After all, it was being treated as a crime scene. He returned to the car.

'Alright. I want to have a look inside while we're here. I shouldn't be too long. You can hop out and stretch your legs, but you can't wander off. I know you were counting on having a bit of a look around, but that's the best I can do for this visit. It's a crime scene, and that bloke's job is to make sure it stays secure. It's pretty much the car park and nothing else for now. Okay?'

'We won't be hopping out. There's no spirits here. Beverly told me already.'

Tahlia looked grim. Rory was non-plussed to silence, briefly.

'Alright then. I'll try not to be long.'

First impressions were of a museum. An era preserved. The massive hallway and two front reception rooms were well furnished, without being over-furnished, with a collection of dark carved timber bureaus, tables, upholstered formal chairs and glass cabinets. Floral and Persian rugs stretched the breadth of each room. Nothing offered comfort until deeper in the house. In a well-used snug with a television set, two comfortable viewing chairs had worn well beyond that point. Rory crossed the hallway to a study. It too appeared well used … or at least well searched. The door of a large safe was ajar, as were those of tall glass built-in cabinets with drawers. The leather insert of the main desk was barely visible under documents, and lever arch files were piled on it and on a corner table. Rory scanned the uppermost of those — mainly accounts and bank statements, no actual correspondence. He pulled a volume from two shelves of blank spines. It was a 1938 diary. A random page was full of nearly decipherable scrawl about a week of sheep washing. He cringed at the thought of someone having to wade their way through the collection.

Limited free wall space in the study allowed only one picture. Rory immediately recognised the scene in a pencil sketch framed behind glass. It was the stand of she-oak trees and the rolling dale beyond. The artist inscription on the sketch itself told him as much.

THE SHE-OAKS. WHERE KILMANY WAS WON, 1842
Fear where ye tread, on this land once red

Rory looked at the sketch for a long time. A talented amateur, he decided. The artist's small corner signature all but confirmed it. "Isabel Claymore". He took a photograph.

Chapter 31

'If this chook doesn't start doing the speed limit, I'm putting the lights and siren on.'

Rory leaned over to see what the speed Cockburn was doing.

'Shit, Gary. She's doing fifty-eight in a sixty zone. You'll scare the shit out of her. What's the panic?'

'It just shits me. They have speed signs for a reason, you know.'

'Yeah. As a maximum! It's not a minimum.'

They were weaving their way through Melbourne's northern suburbs to the police forensic centre. Rory moved the conversation to matters at hand.

'Are you still holding Claymore in Hamilton, or are you bringing him into Melbourne remand.'

'We're keeping him down there for now. The silly old bastard wanted to know why they wouldn't let him wander down the street to buy a paper.'

'How was he when you brought him in?'

'Quiet but seething. Denying everything.'

'Is his legal rep any good?'

'Top notch. The local cops told me he got lawyered up properly when his wife left him. Being fucking rich also helps.'

'When you say he denied everything, do you mean he denied killing her, or he denied going to Sydney.'

'The whole lot. To paraphrase his solicitor: "It never happened. So, there's another XJ Jaguar in Australia. It might be a prestige car, but we're not talking Rolls Royce Silver Ghosts. The *unadulterated* image is so black and white and grainy, you can't tell if it's even the same colour". You get the gist?'

'Yeah. Thank God he didn't get bail.'

'For now. You've got a fucking lot riding on these forensics.'

'We'll see,' Rory answered without taking Cockburn's bait that this was all on Rory.

Cockburn took his eyes off the road to read Rory.

'What are you holding back? I want all our cards on the table when we interview Claymore. If there's anything else, you need to tell me now.'

'There's nothing you don't already know, or have you forgotten that Claymore is of interest in relation to Ricky Lock's disappearance?'

'Oh, I know about your suspicious missing person case, the one you don't seem to have a body for if that's what you mean. Just because you've drawn a blank doesn't mean you can use Claymore's interview as a fishing expedition for a crime that may or may not even exist. For all you know, he could be smoking dope on a beach in Queensland. There's absolutely nothing concerning Ricky Lock's disappearance that links it to Gloria Vella's murder.'

'I think we're about to expose a previously unrecorded massacre of Aborigines that took place on Claymore's property in 1842.'

Cockburn's head swivelled to face Rory again.

'Eighteen-fucking-forty-two! For Christ's sake Rory. You're talking what ... two centuries ago? It was probably legal back then. Tell the historians about it or let the local mob put up a plaque. It's not our business. Claymore did not kill Gloria Vella because Ricky Lock was going to expose some historical transgression that happened on Claymore's land. I've met Claymore. If his ancestors were involved, he'd probably be proud of the fact, which may or may not also be a crime these days, but it's not the one we're dealing with. Ricky Lock. Gloria Vella. Separate cases.'

Cockburn's rant produced silence for the remainder of the trip. When they reached the carpark, Rory made no move to open the car door. Cockburn noticed.

'What? Are you sulking?' he asked.

'I'll make a deal with you. If we go in there and forensics give us a silver bullet, you take all the credit, but you let me dig deeper when we interview Claymore. If there's no coup de grâce, we play it your way.'

'If we walk out of here with a guaranteed conviction, you're on,' Cockburn answered.

Helen de Vries greeted them in a lab coat and led them into the large workshop that housed Claymore's Jaguar.

'We didn't do so well with the rope,' she told them as they followed her to the Jag. 'Although we can prove the obvious, that the rope in Claymore's shed and the rope used in wrapping the body are of the same manufacture, putting them under the microscope didn't shed any light on whether they are from the same spool. There's no telling how many other spools rolled off the same production line. Nevertheless, in this neck of the woods, it is a relatively rare breed. Still, we can't vouch for it being absolutely unique.'

They had come to a stop beside the Jag. Rory and Cockburn looked at each other.

'What's the story here, then?' Rory asked.

'The good news is, we know this is a boot that has had at least one body in it. We can tell that because no one made an attempt to clean the boot after the body was transported in there. Normally that would be a good thing, but in this case, the opposite is the case.'

Suddenly Cockburn and Rory were on the same side.

'I hate it when she strings it out like this. It isn't an Agatha Christie novel, Helen,' Cockburn said.

'We are showing our age, Detective Sergeant. However, in this case, there's a story you need to know and tell if you're going to rely on the evidence.'

Cockburn rolled his eyes.

'One of the bodies we know was transported in this boot was a sheep.'

Helen smiled.

'You are enjoying this,' Cockburn said.

'I fib you not. As far as we can tell, which is pretty far, Claymore had a sheep in here and a live breathing, pissing and shitting sheep. It was probably one he noticed was in strife when he was driving about in his "good" vehicle.'

'Oh fuck,' Cockburn said.

'And that wiped out any forensic trace of Gloria Vella that may have lingered in the boot?' Rory concluded.

Helen cocked her head and adopted a serious expression.

'You would have thought so,' she teased.

'Well?' said Cockburn. 'You don't have to keep milking it.'

'Patience, Detective Sergeant. This is the important bit.'

She opened the boot.

'See the way the boot lid is constructed? Particularly the bracing struts. You'll see they're made of folded metal that is fitted to the lid panel itself. When I say fitted, I don't mean the bracing struts are fastened to the underside of the lid panel along their whole length. It may appear that way because it is such a close fit, but here, and here,' she pointed, 'you'll see there are a couple of lengthy gaps. That gap may only be wide enough for a sheet of paper to pass through, but it's a gap nevertheless.'

'Milking it, Helen.'

This time Helen rolled *her* eyes … and continued.

'You'll also notice the gap narrows to a tight, seamless fit at either end. That means, if something fine enough to find itself in that gap is moved sideways, it will become jammed — jammed so tightly that it will break off rather than become free. Of course, when that happens, the piece that breaks off is jammed so tightly that no amount of cleaning of sheep thrashing about is going to dislodge it. Is it?'

'I think this is where you tell us what got jammed under the strut.'

'You only had to wait. It was a hair. The human hair of a woman.'

'Well done, Helen. You've managed to have us hanging by a single thread. Have you extracted DNA from that thread yet?' Rory asked.

'Funny you should ask. The DNA of the hair matched Gloria Vella's DNA.'

'Is this absolute? One tiny hair sample jammed tightly between two bits of sheet metal. Can this be challenged and shot down in court?' Cockburn asked.

'Safe as houses, Detective Sergeant. When Gloria Vella's hair brushed up against this strut seam, more than one hair managed to become caught. We extracted several … I just thought the story sounded more dramatic with one. Don't worry, this is as solid as DNA evidence gets.'

'Yes!' Cockburn did a fist pump.

'Don't forget the bigger picture here. This boot in front of you is where Gloria Vella died. She was alive when she went in here but not when she came out. She was probably conscious for some of that time and moved about in panic or trying to get the lid to open. That's when her hair would have got caught where it did. That's how she contributed to whatever justice is awaiting her.'

Cockburn and Rory conjured the sobering mental image of Gloria's final journey.

Chapter 32

Alone in a car with Cockburn for four hours. Then, once the job was done, facing an additional four inescapable hours of exasperation for the return journey.

Rory had missed the opportunity to fly to Hamilton ... by thirty years or more. When the nation rode on the sheep's back, Ansett Australia kicked off their airline with none other than a commercial service from Melbourne to the wool capital of Victoria. Now, years after the education of international students took over as the state's top exporter, even the passenger train has stopped going there.

The town nevertheless kept its wool ethos alive with a word they invented and made their own — "Sheepvention". The annual exhibition manages to pull in 20,000 visitors. Less successful was their crack at something big. With The Big Merino already taken by Goulburn in New South Wales, they opted for The Big Wool Bales instead — a wool bale being nothing more inspiring than a rectangular cube. Not even kitsch. Needless to say, it ended up being upcycled.

'I think Natalie should come too,' Rory had suggested.

Problem solved. Natalie kept the nemeses off each other's nerves throughout the trip and during the evening meal they shared at the motel. They were fresh and ready when they fronted up to interview Claymore.

Claymore was also ready. Someone had talked him into changing defence-lawyer horses — from good to very good. Someone had also talked Victor Black into setting aside the comfort of his present-day managing, mentoring and senior partnering role to take on an actual case again.

Gentlemanly, Victor chose to wait in the official interview room for his client and his client's interrogators to arrive. He looked as comfortable there as he would sitting at his Melbourne desk, peering down Port Phillip Bay to its heads from his thirty-first-floor eyrie. A visit to a country police station was no pretext for Victor to dress down however. He wore his usual office clobber — an understated suit, white shirt and blue tie. Black framed spectacles added thoughtfulness to his cropped grey beard and un-thinning grey hair. Charm came naturally … scruples were a different matter.

He politely asked for more time with his client before they began. Cockburn, Rory and Natalie found themselves standing and waiting in the corridor.

'Take your time,' Cockburn had said as they left. Nothing like signalling we may have something up our sleeve, Rory thought.

Finally, they were all seated, and the preliminaries of recording dealt with. Cockburn and Rory facing Claymore and Victor. Natalie was outside the room, observing and taking notes. Claymore sat stoically as Cockburn kicked things off.

'Mr Claymore, we wanted to ask you some more questions regarding one of the charges against you, specifically, the murder of Gloria Vella.'

Victor jumped in before Cockburn could begin his first question.

'For the record, Detective Sergeant Cockburn, let me reiterate that my client denies knowing Ms Vella, let alone murdering her. He also refutes that the car you have video footage of near Ms Vella's residence could possibly be his own. I say that so you don't spend time asking my client questions he has already provided answers for to the best of his knowledge and ability. Unless, of course, we are here to dispense with the matter altogether.'

Cockburn gave an amused smile.

'Well, I'm afraid I have one more question about Mr Claymore's vehicle. I apologise for not covering this in our last interview, but at that stage, the results of the forensic examination of your client's Jaguar were not at hand.' He shifted his attention to ask Claymore directly.

'Mr Claymore. How do you explain the presence of DNA material belonging to Ms Vella in the boot of your Jaguar? Specifically, several strands of her hair.'

The room paused. Rory thought he heard the beep, beep, beep of a truck reversing somewhere distant. Claymore looked pleadingly at Victor.

'Can we pause the interview, please, so I can consult my client about how he wishes to proceed?'

'We're not in court yet, Mr Black. Still … I'm happy to go and get a coffee,' Cockburn said, cranking his glee up a notch.

Coffee turned into sandwiches for lunch before Victor Black had charted a way forward for Elliot Claymore.

They reassembled, and Cockburn hit Record. The performance began with Victor.

'My client continues to deny murdering Gloria Vella. He does, however, acknowledge that Ms Vella was in the boot of his car for a period, so he may have been guilty of unintentional deprivation of her liberty … or something along those lines.'

Victor was still doing his best to paint the whole thing as trivial.

'Well, seeing as there's no such charge as "unintentional deprivation of liberty", why don't we hear what your client has to say, and we'll decide whether there's a reason why we shouldn't continue to prosecute your client for murder?'

'Then I re-reiterate, you have my client's position on record that he did not murder Gloria Vella. That remains unchanged.'

Cockburn gave Victor his best ray, then began.

'Mr Claymore. How did Gloria Vella end up in the boot of your car?'

Victor gave him the nod to answer as they had discussed.

'I did it to get back at Travis Vella and Eva.'

'Who is Eva?' Cockburn jumped in.

'My ex-wife. I saw her and that mining leech, Vella, together. She must have been the one feeding information to him. There's no way I was having Kilmany dug up. It's been in my family's hands since before Victoria was even created. Vella had the nerve to bring his crew onto the place and start doing stuff, even after I declined his unsolicited and unwelcome approach. He clearly wasn't going to take no for an answer.'

'Were you stalking your ex-wife, Mr Claymore,' Rory asked.

Claymore looked at Victor. They whispered, and Victor answered.

'They live near a small town. It's hard for my client not to see people he knows when he's out and about.'

Rory rolled his eyes. 'So, how did you know about Gloria Vella, Mr Claymore?'

'I didn't know her. I knew he wore a wedding ring, and I knew where he lived. The address was on the mail in his ute. I couldn't tackle him directly without copping suspicion because, as you know, we had already rigorously crossed swords. But I do know what it was like to suffer having your wife leave. I thought maybe that was something I could … facilitate. See how he dealt with that kind of loss. I mean, she was in Sydney. No one was going to point the finger at anyone this far away.'

'So, you did intend to kill her?' Cockburn said.

'That's not what my client actually said. When he makes a comparison with his own situation, we both know he is not talking about murdering someone. Eva Claymore is very much still alive.'

'Then let me spell it out more clearly. And Mr Black, please let your client answer the question himself.'

Cockburn fixed his eyes back on Claymore.

'You've told us: for the sake of vengeance, you drove all the way to Sydney to "facilitate" Mr Vella losing his wife. That leaves the undeniable conclusion that your purpose was to kill Mrs Vella. Was that not the case, Mr Claymore?'

'That's not what happened,' Claymore said.

'My client …' Victor began to say. Cockburn cut him off.

'My client. My client. You have lots of clients. Why don't we stick with Elliot Claymore … and let him answer the question himself?'

'Whatever you like, Detective Sergeant Cockburn. Please continue, Elliot.'

'I didn't know what I was going to do when I went to her house. When I started telling her how angry I was with Travis Vella, she scoffed and told me he was seeing someone else. They would probably end up divorced. He wouldn't have given two hoots what happened to her. I'd probably be doing him a favour. That annoyed me even more. I'd gone all that way.'

It had come to the bit where Claymore had to admit what he did. He dropped his gaze to continue.

'I might have lost it a bit, only verbally at that stage. Then she lost it back at me — shouting. We were standing at her back door, and neighbours could hear. I had to shut her up. I instinctively hit her. She fell like a sack of wheat, but she wasn't dead. Not even unconscious. She was groggy, dazed maybe, but at least she'd shut up.'

'There was a decent knock on her head, but no blood was found at the house. How did that happen?' Cockburn asked.

'By then, she knew who I was, so I panicked. That's when I put her in the boot. I knocked her head, getting her into the boot. And then I drove. I never figured out what to do. I just drove.'

'We know you drove. You had at least an eleven-hour drive ahead of you. How long was it before you opened the boot, Mr Claymore ... or did you think she was dead already from the knock on her head?'

Victor touched Claymore on the forearm again.

'I think Elliot should take his time answering this question ... it was a while ago, and some details might not spring to mind immediately. Like, did he take the opportunity to allow fresh air into the boot during any number of possible breaks? A rest, toilet, buying petrol, food. Maybe all of those things.'

'Well, whatever answer Mr Claymore's chooses to give, based on those kind suggestions, is pretty much academic,' Cockburn said sarcastically. 'The pathologist has determined exactly how long Gloria lasted without the boot being opened. Do you want to know how long it takes to suffocate in your old Jag XJ boot, Mr Claymore? There's not as much space in those things as you'd expect. The spare tyre, battery and petrol tank are all packed in there, in what is an entirely compartmentalised section of the chassis. So, it's pretty much airtight, I'd say. Even so, the pathologist tells us it would take at least seventeen hours for Gloria to die.'

Claymore dropped his head. Cockburn didn't allow him to dwell.

'You knew what to do when you thought it was safe to open the boot, though, didn't you, Mr Claymore?'

Claymore seemed relieved to get back to telling his story unabashed.

'That bit was easy. When I realised she'd died, I had to find somewhere to bury her. I thought there'd be a hole already dug at the gem site, and I wasn't wrong. There was no one around, and there, on the edge of the site, was the deepest, abandoned hole I'd ever seen, just waiting, ready. I covered her well before I left. A metre or two of clay, I reckon. I left the rest of the job to whoever looks after the place.

'I mean, I didn't plan for any of that to happen, but it did the job in the end … without me actually killing her. You and everyone else thought her husband had killed her. That's not how I meant to get at Vella, but he did suffer. Your lot and the media made sure of that.'

Victor touched Claymore's arm before he strayed incriminatingly off script.

Rory didn't want Claymore's outpouring to wind down.

'Mr Claymore, what happened when a young guy called Ricky came to Kilmany about three years ago?'

Victor swung his head to look at Claymore. Claymore held his hand to Victor's ear and whispered.

'We'd like another break, please.'

'Last break. After this, you just answer the questions.'

'Are you done?' Rory asked Cockburn once in the hallway.

'I am, as it happens. And thanks for leaving it until now to check.'

'I didn't want to lose momentum.'

'Well, he's all yours. You've started this fiasco. Now let's see you get yourself out.'

'My client does not recall anyone by the name of Ricky.'

'What happened when Cecil Gaynor and Lenny Dalton came to see you before Ricky did?' Rory asked. 'And before you jump in, Mr Black, we know Mr Claymore met both men because he took the trouble of having one of his other lawyers send them a letter about the matter.'

Victor gestured to Claymore to enlighten Rory … and perhaps himself.

'Those … stains on society …' He spat the words. '… stood on my doorstep and cast aspersions upon my ancestors. If you've already spoken to them, they would have told you they got the short shrift they deserved. And as for that Gaynor, his father married one of them.'

'When you say "one of them", you mean Aboriginal, don't you, Mr Claymore.'

'If you want to use a polite term. I knew what they were up to, though. They create a story like that, and the next thing you know, they'd be seeking native title for the whole place. It needed to be nipped in the bud, and it was. My ancestors fought for Kilmany, and I'm not having their lot wander back in, thinking they can lay claim on any of the place.'

'That was the basis of why they came to see you, wasn't it, Mr Claymore?'

'What do you mean?'

'Like you said, your ancestors fought the original inhabitants. Cecil Gaynor had uncovered a family record that said Aborigines were massacred by the settlers on Kilmany, and they were buried there. That's what they spoke to you about.'

'I think you'll find that Mr Gaynor is not able to produce that record. They have no legitimate claim on Kilmany.'

Rory noted that Claymore's answer intimated that the record had, in fact, existed. *Was it enough to bring possible arson of Cecil Gaynor's house into play? Not without some evidence*, Rory decided in his head. The moment or two of thought passed before Rory continued.

'I'm surprised you believe, falsely as it happens, that native title claims can be made for freehold land, but that's another matter.'

Claymore looked at Victor, who gave a nod to confirm Rory was right. Rory continued.

'And you're wrong about there being no record of the massacre. This record has been in your family for nearly 180 years.'

Rory retrieved the small Kilmany she-oak sketch from a bag at his feet. Its inscription said it all:

THE SHE-OAKS. WHERE KILMANY WAS WON, 1842
Fear where ye tread, on this land once red

'Here it is, hidden in plain view, a clear record for the knowledge of each successive generation. Where the skeletons, literally, are hidden. Perhaps family folklore has also been handed down the line. Maybe it cracks a mention in those diaries we'll be looking at.'

As intrigued as Victor was finding the dialogue, he knew an allegation when he heard one.

'It sounds like you're making an allegation yourself, Detective Sergeant James.'

'It's no allegation, Mr Black. Ground-penetrating radar, as inexact as it can be, has revealed the presence of what we believe are the bones of multiple humans at this very site. The site where Mr Claymore found Travis Vella's assistant using seismic equipment, in the mistaken belief he was in Mr Claymore's neighbour's paddock.'

Claymore slammed the table with his fist and leant forward with anger.

'That was no mistake … and I caught Vella's offsider just in time. Eva knew about that paddock, and she was playing Vella. You don't know what she's like. She's still got her claws into me … trying to get more land her lawyers tell her she's entitled to. She would have had the place mined just to spite me. Pure spite. Having the massacre exposed to blacken the Claymore name would have been cream on the top for her.'

Victor looked to Rory to explain.

'Mr Claymore put an axe into the seismic reader being used by one of Mr Vella's employees. The Eva conspiracy is in Mr Claymore's head. Eva was with a friend of Travis when they bumped into each other in the street one day. That was the entire extent of his connection with Mrs Claymore.'

'I believe she's gone back to being Eva Clancy,' Victor corrected him.

'She couldn't wait,' Claymore spat. 'And you …' he demanded, waving a hostile finger at Rory. 'What right do you have to come on to Kilmany and start probing the place with seismic equipment?'

'You know we have a search warrant.'

He turned on Victor.

'Is that bloody true? That the search warrant lets them do that? You never told me they'd be searching the land. Under the land. You said they didn't need to know anything about the fucking massacre.'

Rory didn't want Claymore distracted.

'I'll ask you again, Mr Claymore. What happened when Ricky showed up?'

Claymore's ferocity wasn't dissipating.

'I'll tell you what happened. The same thing that has happened to anyone like that since Kilmany was settled. The Claymores fought them then, and we'll fight them now.'

'By them, you mean Aboriginal, don't you, Mr Claymore? In effect, you're now telling us that Ricky Lock — who moments ago you said you have no knowledge of — did show up at Kilmany. You did encounter him. That's how you do know him and why you now refer to him as Aboriginal.'

Victor put his hand on Claymore's forearm again.

'STOP PUTTING YOUR FUCKING HAND ON MY ARM, YOU HABEAS CORPUS BLOODSUCKING

FLEABAG,' he shouted. 'They've got you convinced freehold land is off-limits for native title. How long would that hold for a massacre site? As far as I'm concerned, you can go and sit on their side of the table. Everyone else in the country is caving to black armband cliques. When this country was there to be won, there were some real cops around who knew what side their bread was buttered. They knew how to dispense summary justice to deal with the black menace our ancestors faced. And they earned praise for it from those who mattered. People with the courage to enter this wilderness and make something of it. You check your history. You'll see I'm right. Not everything needed to be swept under the carpet.'

By the end of his rant, Claymore was on his feet. He slammed a boot into his chair and broke its leg.

'Don't bother getting me another one. You can stick this interview up your collective arseholes.'

If anyone had reason to "check your history", as Claymore yelled, they would have learnt how wretchedly true his rant was. In the 1840s, Captain Henry Dana was commandant of a crack squad that hunted down groups of sheep-stealing Aborigines in western Victoria, with a take-no-prisoners MO. Demoralising for participants on both sides of battle was the mounted-police troop's inclusion of Kulin nation Aborigines from around Melbourne. The one-sided rifles-versus-spears carnage earned Dana widespread praise from newspapers and squatters.

On the return journey, they changed drivers at Skipton. Rory took over the wheel, Cockburn pulled rank for the front passenger seat. Natalie retreated to the rear.

'Bad luck the shutters went up on Ricky Lock, Rory.'

'D'ya reckon, Natalie? I can't say I was surprised. For a racist old bastard, most of the time he's pretty careful about what he admits out loud. Even when he rants.'

'Yeah, well, maybe he keeps the worst of his racism for the doing. There's not much doubt in my mind that he had everything to do with Ricky going missing.'

'Hmm. Not much use without a body or a crime to charge him with.'

'Cheer up, laughing boy. At least you can tell your little archaeologist mate that Claymore'll be doing major time. By the time I'm done nailing him for Gloria Vella, he won't be seeing his precious Kilmany again in his own lifetime.'

'It will do him in when that reality sinks in, but it'll be little consolation for Tahlia and her mum. Not unless Ricky's body is found. That's what's important to them,' Rory said.

'What about doing a deal on the charges ... if he comes clean on Ricky Lock?' Natalie asked.

'No fucking way,' Cockburn said, already making Natalie feel foolish for asking. 'To begin with, Claymore's not going to stick his hand up for another murder when he thinks he has a chance of getting the Gloria Vella charge downgraded. I know that if Victor Black still has a client and has his druthers, he'd be shooting for false imprisonment ... bypassing manslaughter altogether. But you think about it, Natalie. You don't leave a person in a car boot for more than seventeen hours by accident. It's a deliberate act. The only way he could argue manslaughter is to say he knocked her head accidentally when he was putting her in the boot, and he thought she was already dead when he closed the boot. And even if the blow was accidental, he still did it in the process of what? Kidnapping her to do away with her — there's no other way to interpret that action. The motive and premeditation is still there. There's no way I'll be settling for manslaughter. Not even if he did come clean on Ricky Lock.'

'None of it's your call, though, is it?' Rory said.

'My case. My win. My conviction. My stat. Don't you remember our conversation in the Forensic Centre carpark?'

'That was before we knew where the murder took place. On the face of Claymore's account, the murder was committed in New South Wales. You might be handing the whole thing over to Rochelle Oglethorpe. You got on well with her, didn't you? Maybe she'll buy you a slab — of Tooheys.'

'But ...' Cockburn instinctively knew that he was having none of it. It nevertheless took him a beat to produce a reason why. 'The pathologist's report says she lasted at least seventeen hours. He would have been well over the Murray River by the time she carked it. Nice try, Rory.'

'What about that motel receipt on the New South Wales file? The one where Claymore stayed overnight on his way back from Sydney.' Natalie said. 'I might be wrong because I haven't lived in this country as long as you fellas, but isn't West Wyalong in New South Wales?'

A surprised Rory took his eyes from the road to glance over his shoulder at Natalie. She winked.

Cockburn thumped the glovebox with the base of both palms. Then he did it again … and again.

'Fuck, fuck, fuck.'

Chapter 33

The line from a Ricky Nelson song, "I went to a garden party", sprang to Rory's mind. Of course, the sentiment of the 1970s rock and roll lament couldn't have been less germane. Maybe it was because Rory suspected the presence of some dissembling attitudes, just as Ricky Nelson — by then, he'd outgrown being Ricky — rued in his sardonic lyrics. "*Ya can't please everyone, so ya got to please yourself*".

Notwithstanding that Rory was standing in a paddock rather than a garden per se, the first white man to clap eyes on the place — the seemingly ubiquitous Major — surely begged to differ. He described the neck of the woods as "a nobleman's park on a gigantic scale". With all the hallmarks in place for the day, it did indeed resemble a garden party of the grandest order. Professional event organisers had been engaged to make it so.

An open-sided marquee accommodated cloth-covered tables, soon to be laden with bush tucker. Oversized floral centrepieces were all native f lora — bold banksia spikes, gum flowers, wattle and foliage. The marquee was served by a caterer's tent, drinks tent, refrigerated van, and a buzzing coffee van. Carparking and two portaloos were on the upside, ensuring the lawn-like vista of pasture and noble red-gums rolled uninterrupted to the west horizon.

Some body-painted dancers who would later perform gathered in a group among the modest Indigenous and non-Indigenous crowd. The real star of the occasion, however, was a veiled rock monument, set apart behind a microphone on a stand and flanked by pole-mounted speakers.

An unmistakable scent alerted those present that formalities would soon commence — the smell of tinder-dry eucalypt leaves and twigs being set alight. Two men had begun preparing for the welcome-to country smoking ceremony. They allowed dry sticks to gather flame and heat. The smoke-producing green leaves would remain in a pile beside the fire until the master-of-ceremonies stepped up to the microphone.

The emcee was the CEO of one of the Aboriginal cooperatives. His relatively young years rendered him more a mover and shaker within his own circles than an elder. The co-operative's logo was embroidered on the navy fleece vest he wore over his khaki shirt and strides. He cued green leaves to be added to the fire and proceeded to introduce the smoking ceremony. Then the suits got their go. Top of the list was a state minister. Local government, state government, the federal government were all represented, as were some aspiring candidates for the next parliamentary election.

A gentler tone was struck when an elder spoke in language. The dancers performed to their own clapped rhythm and chants before the MC returned to address the matter at hand — the unveiling. Before he called upon elders to do that, he announced there were two more people to thank. The first of those was Eva Clancy. Eva had indeed acquired the land in her protracted settlement with Elliot Claymore. She would be donating the site to the local Aboriginal community. People clapped.

The MC became even more solemn when he said he wanted to thank Ricky Lock from Bundjalung country.

'Ricky, in his thorough quest to discover and divulge the very existence of this sacred place, is no longer with us,' the MC said. 'It was Ricky Lock and Tahlia Lock in her mission to find her brother Ricky, who awakened us, and the world, to this site. To this injustice. It was Ricky who led us all here.'

He looked skyward and said he hoped Ricky was here today, then gestured Tahlia to the microphone. He lowered it for her and stepped back. Tahlia stilled herself, brought her thoughts to bear, and began to sing without accompaniment.

> Let me take you home, to your own country
> To Bundjalung land, by the rivers and sea
> Let the wind speed your soul, across the sky
> And lay you to rest, where the sea eagles fly.

Tahlia ended with the breeze whispering through the she-oak needles. People knew not to applaud. Holding back tears was a different matter.

Rory waited for the dignitaries to do group photos and for the throng to return to the marquees. He made his way to the rock. The brass plaque told him that at least fifteen souls lay beneath. Killed in 1842, as the inscription on Claymore's sketch had attested. Actual musket shot and musket shot damaged bones detected by Travis Vella's ground-penetrating radar revealed the mode of death — at the hands of the European landholders. Rory knew the number killed was greater, but the radar had its limitations. Only one small dig was undertaken to sample and verify the authenticity of the bones. The final acknowledgement on the plaque did, however, give Rory solace.

"... to Ricky Lock, Bundjalung man, for leading us here."

Tahlia joined him. They looked at the plaque together. Tahlia was first to stir. Rory turned and saw the smoky quartz crystal she wore on a fine leather neck strap. She noticed him notice it.

'Terry's partner Rose gave it to me. I had it mounted to wear for Ricky. It seemed right.'

'Very,' he said. 'And I see your mum is here today. I presume she's proud.'

'Proud and sad. More sad than proud, actually. She wants me to thank you.'

Rory shrugged. 'I'm with your mum. This is momentous for the local clan but no consolation as far as Ricky is concerned. I'm really sorry we didn't get there, Tahlia.'

'I'll still be looking. Travis said he'll bring the ground-penetrating radar gear back if we find any likely signs.'

'So he should. Travis Vella owes his freedom to you. If you hadn't shown up on the scene, Cockburn would have had him doing time by now.'

'That's scary.'

'I know. And I have to work with him.'

The fire tenders began to build the fire beside them.

'Looks like they're settling in for the night,' Rory observed.

'They are. This day-time session has been to tell the world. To let them know these things can't be swept under the carpet forever. But the carnival will be packed up and outta here by sundown. That's when the local mob will be honouring their ancestors properly. That's when they'll have this place to themselves. After that, there'll be no signs or fingerboards telling people how to get here. This will be their place.'

There was nothing for Rory to say. They both reflected more on the plaque.

'You know, the first time we met, you sang …' Rory pondered, without finishing the thought.

She turned to him inquiringly.

'I thought I was going to carry Ricky with me as a burden. That can happen with unsolved cases. But after hearing you sing today, it's …'

He gestured with his hands for a word.

'Shared,' she said. And smiled.

301

DYING FOR
A COFFEE

Several historic buildings could be dubbed the pride of View Street, but for Detective Sergeant Rory James, that honour always sat with the Wine Bank cafe. The grand former bank—one of six uphill of Charing Cross—served what Rory swore was the best coffee in Bendigo. Its Corinthian columns may have been fewer and a tad shorter than the Capital Theatre's, but the Wine Bank's beckoning aromas led him blinkered past rival splendours. He hunkered on under threatening cloud and fast-ebbing willpower.

Plainly, website writers who insisted Sigrid Dobell's "The Manse" B&B was within easy walking distance of the View Street cafes had never spent the night going toe-to-toe with Sigrid through a bottle of single malt. Avoiding a pain-steeped morning recovery expedition was as inconceivable as cars making a comeback in Hargreaves Mall. Moreover, he avoided graver impairment by not staying put and ingesting the brake fluid taste-alike that Sigrid passed off as coffee.

Rory stood watching the Wine Bank owner place a CLOSED signboard at the entrance. Rain arrived on cue and song lyrics, near tailored for the moment, spilled from the café sound system.

Standing at Charing Cross in the rain ...

His misery was un-ignorable. The owner offered a what-can-you-do shrug.

'Sorry mate. The cops have shut us down. We found dead bodies inside.'

Survival kicked in ahead of disbelief. 'Is the coffee machine still on?' Rory rasped.

'Nah, and I couldn't make you one if it was. There really are two dead bodies. This place will be crawling with cops.'

'Where *are* these cops then?'

'To tell the truth, that bit really pisses me off. Plumbers found the bodies—and a basement we never knew we had — while they were replacing a burst pipe. Nothing grizzly though ... it's like they've been there forever. Borderline archaeological I reckon. The cops ordered a special forensic team from Melbourne, strung up crime scene tape, then bolted. Dunno when they'll show up.' He repeated the what-can-you-do gesture. 'Bastards. You can tell they've never been in business.'

'Turn the coffee machine back on and give me a look.'

The owner's bemusement hung.

'I'm a homicide cop. Detective Sergeant Rory James …
from Melbourne,' he saw fit to add. He showed his ID.

'Am I allowed to do that?' he asked Rory.

'You're not allowed not to, including not turning the
coffee machine on. Now, what's your name?'

'Mark Coffey.'

Rory hesitated a beat, then decided not to expend pre-
coffee words clarifying if that was a barista's real surname.

'Just show me the bodies,' he said.

They stared into the unwelcome abyss in the café floor. A
massive sheet of slate flagstones, fixed together on the
underside, had been lifted at one end and propped with a
solid length of timber. Rory pointed to the unlit tradie light
dangling at the end of a yellow extension cord — word free
communication of the coffee-deprived.

'I'll turn it on,' Mark twigged. He found the switch and
began showing Rory.

'There's this bloke here, sort of crumpled below where
they lifted the slate. His mate's sitting against the back wall.
And here's the thing, there's no way in or out. The other
cops, sorry police, were totally baffled.'

The next track kicked in on the café speakers:

No fortune to be made, Gold filled these shallow graves.

'You want me to turn that off? Penny plays it when she's
cleaning up the kitchen.'

'Just make sure she's got the coffee machine on.'

Rory somehow descended to his knees with the speed —
if that's not the wrong word — of a praying mantis on dope.

He scanned the underside of the flagstones for a good
while before taking in the scene below. The chalky brick-
lined space was too small to be a usable room. It was also too
low to stand in without stooping. The figures were skeletal
but still draped in their clothes. One had indeed accepted his
fate sitting against the back wall. The other body was a
contorted heap below the opening. The floor, and some
indiscernible debris, was black with damp from the leak.
Higher up, the dust laden bodies and walls had morphed to a
uniform light-grey.

'The plumbers reckon rats got into them. This bloke has
had fingers chewed off one hand.'

'Hmm. Did you have any idea this cavity existed?'

'Shit no. I spent a lot of time and money restoring the
place myself and I can tell you it's not on the old plans. And I
don't think the National Trust knew about it. They bought
and owned the building for a long while after the ANZ
branch closed in the nineteen-seventies. It's probably a
basement remnant from the original chambers they knocked
down to create this classic in the *eighteen*-seventies.'

Money goes out quicker than it comes in ... That's our
cash grab.

Rory noticed the band had added horns and Hammond
organ on this track, evoking the might of Bruce Springsteen's
E Street Band.

'Who's the band …' he asked Penny as she came past with a bag of rubbish, '…and have you got that coffee machine going?'

'It's the Four Lions. Their "Vahland" album, I think. Fiercely-local musos if you hadn't guessed … and yeah, the machines' warming up.'

Rory gave an unsmiling thumb-up and turned back to Mark.

'Anything else you can tell me about when the place was being built?'

'Not really. You won't find much in the archives either because the builder shot through a day or two before the bank moved in. It must have been one of those jobs that sends a builder broke. These slate flagstones for instance were literally worth their weight in gold. The whole lot was brought from England as ships' ballast. When it was offloaded in Port Melbourne, they restored the ship's balance for the return journey with vaultfuls of Bendigo gold.'

Rory unfolded his body from its kneeling position even more slowly than he'd gone down. He continued studying the subterranean scene as he thought aloud.

'I reckon Penny's Four Lions nailed it. This was an attempted *cash grab*. These blokes went in there intending to emerge a couple of nights after the bank moved in and help themselves. And it has to be your missing builder. No one else would have access to the space, or know it even existed. Trouble was, one of them got his hand caught under the slate as they lowered it. It would have been too heavy for the other bloke to lift it off on his own … they died trapped in a soundproof tomb. The body of this poor bugger eventually fell away from his fingers. They're still up here.'

He pointed.

Mark bent under the propped sheet of slate. The white insides of four finger bones were adhered to its underside lip. They had split apart like pea shells when the slate was lifted. No doubt the other half of the finger bones remained fixed to the ledge where the slate had rested for nigh on a century and a half — somewhere under the plumber's mud-caked boot prints.

Mark straightened, clearly impressed. Rory spoke first.

'Now, how about a double-shot long black?'

Acknowledgements and Notes

DEEP DOWN

Thank you to Mary, for everything, *and* for being such an astute content editor. Thanks too to Des Lowry for copyediting. For their review of the manuscript — Dianne Dempsey, Jennie de Jong, Brendan King, Graeme McKechnie, and Gilda McKechnie. For generously sharing their knowledge — Greg McAdam, Roger Hallam, Damien Lehane, Terry Wood, John Latimer, and Brendan King. To Cori Leahy for allowing herself and Grampians Pioneer Cottages to be portrayed fictionally.

I am grateful to Prof Ian Clark for taking the time to read the novel, clarify historical references and offer encouraging praise. Ian is the author of *Scars in the Landscape: A register of massacre sites in western Victoria, 1803-1850*, Australian Institute of Aboriginal and Torres Strait Islander Studies, 1995. The register includes massacres that occurred in the Victoria Range side of the Grampians at the hands of the Native Police Corps, one of which is referenced in the novel's plot. This important publication also mentions that other un-reported massacres took place at the hands of settlers. It explains that there was an unwillingness to detail the violence and that an attitude of silence existed, aimed at preserving the anonymity of those involved. The settler-led massacre portrayed in this novel as having taken place at "Kilmany" is entirely fictitious, as is the property, "Kilmany". Kilmany is, however, the name of a village about fifty kilometres north of Edinburgh in Scotland.

Quotes attributed to Major Thomas Mitchell are from *Three Expeditions into the Interior of Eastern Australia*, 2nd edition, by Major TL Mitchell, T&W Boone, 1839. That account includes his encounter with Aborigines on the Murray River, where seven "treacherous savages" were killed. He then proceeded to cross the Murray, en-route to find the Grampians and much else of the about-to-be-formalised Port Phillip District of New South Wales, later Victoria.

The fictitious character, Senior Constable Damon Rich at Cavendish police station is not based on any actual occupants of that role. The character is entirely the product of the author's imagination and any resemblance to any persons living or dead is coincidental.

As far as was known at the time of writing, the fictional "Vehicle Knowall" prototype app had not yet been conceived, designed or developed.

The Black Range referred to in the novel is the western Black Range, north of Rocklands Reservoir, not the eastern Black Range, south of Stawell.

DYING FOR A COFFEE

Thank you to Amy Doak of Accidental Publishing for commissioning and publishing this short story in the 2019 Bendigo anthology: *Goldfields – A Collection of Treasures by Local Authors*.

The historic crime portrayed in this story, and its perpetrators, are entirely fictitious. The Wine Bank was actually built by the much-respected George Pallett who also built Bendigo's town hall and railway station. Pallett Street in Golden Square is named after him. The Wine Bank architects, Alfred Smith and Arthur Johnson, also designed Melbourne's Supreme Court and St Kilda's famous music venue, the Esplanade "Espy" Hotel. Thank you to Bendigo's fab Four Lions for permission to use their song lyrics. Thank you too to Wine Bank owner, Mark Coffey, for allowing himself to be portrayed fictionally.